PIONEERS *of*
MILL CREEK CANYON

PIONEERS *of*
MILL CREEK CANYON

SHANNON WRAY

THE
History
PRESS

Published by The History Press
Charleston, SC
www.historypress.com

Copyright © 2020 by Shannon Wray
All rights reserved

Front cover, top: Forest Home stage, circa 1890s. Thomas Akers and Richard Jackson standing at far right. Courtesy Archives, A.K. Smiley Public Library; *bottom*: vintage Mill Creek Canyon postcard. Courtesy Archives, A.K. Smiley Public Library.
Back cover: Powell family private collection; *left inset*: courtesy California State Archives; *right inset*: courtesy Archives, A.K. Smiley Public Library.

First published 2020

Manufactured in the United States

ISBN 9781467145336

Library of Congress Control Number: 2020932084

For Hallee and Fraser Fresco
Who keep me mindful of legacies,
and
For Tim Harty
Who said, "Let's go home."

CONTENTS

ACKNOWLEDGEMENTS

First, my gratitude to the people of the communities of Forest Falls, Mountain Home Village and Angelus Oaks, California, who have come to listen to my long tales and whose interest in the history of where they live is raucous and unflagging. The kids at Fallsvale School, who enthusiastically greet "the history lady," give me hope that there will always be curiosity about these beautiful, fragile communities that are also my home.

Foremost, however, I owe an enormous debt of gratitude to the descendants and family members of the pioneers chronicled in this book. Many of them climbed into attics or crawled into basements and storage areas to find the treasures that I sought, or they shared their intimate knowledge. I am humbled by their generosity and willingness. They are the following: Dr. Kim Marcus, Tom Castro, Susan Wyckoff, Mr. and Mrs. David Shaw, Kerry Petersen, David Degraw, Sandra Chase, Norma Harvey, Debra Conn, Mrs. Donna Weppler, Mr. and Mrs. Ben A. Reeves, Tracie Deroche, Kathy Mackrill, Linda C. Driscoll, Joyce Cooley Carvalho, L. Howard Richards, Gina Swank Prather, Gayle Crisfield and especially Janice Gillmore.

The unsung heroes of history, those who care for archives and collections, deserve every praise for their patience and perseverance and for the work they do to ensure that there are stories to tell well into the future. My personal thanks to Nathan Gonzales and Katie Montemayor at the Heritage Room of the A.K. Smiley Public Library; Genevieve Preston and Stanley Rodriguez at the San Bernardino County Historical Archives; Sue Payne at the California Room of the San Bernardino Public Library; Lyn Killian at the San Bernardino Historical and Pioneer Society; Paul Spitzzeri, curator of the Homestead Museum, and his trusty sidekick Alexandra Rasic; John Cahoon at the Seaver Center for Western History Research at the Museum of Natural History in Los Angeles; Elder Johnnie Johnson and the librarians at the Church History Library of the Church of Jesus Christ of Latter-day Saints; Jennifer Williams and Deborah Clifford at the Pomona Valley Historical Society; Molly Haigh in special collections at the Charles E. Young Research Library at UCLA; the hardworking photo specialists at the Huntington Library; Terri Garst and Christina Rice at the Los Angeles Public Library; Yuri Shcherbina at the USC Digital Library; Carol Myers at the San Diego History Center; Jennifer Dickerson at the San Bernardino County Museum; Ed Hume and Jennifer Cusack at Southern California Edison; and all of the other archivists and helping hands who have provided support and content for this book. Astonished thanks to Mark Durban and Sevag and Melissa Baghboudarian at Graphics Designed Ink for going above and beyond.

Very special thanks to Gary and Carol Burgess at Burgess Photographics for their friendship, art, support and enthusiasm for our local history. Thanks, too, to Barbara Becerra for sharing the joy of Mill Creek stories and the hope that all of Forest Home's history will be preserved. Also, my deep gratitude to archaeologists John D. Goodman II, a fellow Fallsvalian, and Gina Griffith for their expert work, and to Tom Atchley.

My sincere respect and appreciation to Ernest and June Siva of the Dorothy Ramon Learning Center in Banning, California; and Clifford Trafzer, distinguished professor of history, and Rupert Costo, chair in American Indian affairs, at the University of California, Riverside. Their graciousness and encouragement made all the difference.

I am so very fortunate to have the gentle guiding hand of an editor who is insightful and positive in Laurie Krill. Sincere appreciation to Rick Delaney for his gifts of clarity and deft editing, too. Thanks also go to Crystal Murray, Joe Gorman, Sarah Haynes and Maddison Potter and the entire team of amazing professionals at The History Press.

Finally, my love and gratitude to my family who nurtured, supported and sacrificed for "the writer"; Phoebe Larmore, literary guardian angel and soul sister; and mountain sister Rebekah Wellman. Without them, my words would never have found their way to these pages.

INTRODUCTION

When we tire of well-worn ways, we seek for new. This restless craving in the souls of men spurs them to climb, and to seek the mountain view.
—Ella Wheeler Wilcox

Mill Creek Canyon in the San Bernardino National Forest of Southern California is a place defined by its history, geology, disasters and "firsts." The stalwart individualists who found their way to the banks of Mill Creek in the early settler history of California were seeking something—a sense of the sacred, an opportunity, an escape, a home or a missing piece of a life. They were adventurers, eccentrics, dreamers, visionaries and builders who lived and worked in the deep, tangled forests along Mill Creek. Each left legacies—some good, some bad, others hilarious, bizarre or sad—and contributed to the growth and character of a place that bears their imprint.

The history of this unique area begins, and will always remain, as the story of the traditional territory of the *Yuhaaviatam* people or "Serrano," as the Spanish named them.[1] It is important to understand that the settler stories told in this book are only a moment in the fullness of time on the land, an imposition on cultures that were extant and evolving for millennia before the arrival of Europeans and Americans. Beyond that, this volume primarily encompasses one hundred years, between 1840 and 1940, and straddles the nineteenth and twentieth centuries. Not because those years were the beginning and the end, by any means, but because they were the

Mill Creek Canyon, circa 1900. *Putnam and Valentine, Los Angeles.*

years when the canyon was seen through the eyes of discovery by those who came to claim it.

Mill Creek Canyon is a twelve-mile-long, steep, dead-end box canyon nestled in the San Bernardino Mountains. It was formed by seismic activity and by erosion from twenty or so occasional and year-round creeks that feed the main channel of Mill Creek, which runs down the center.[2] The area boasts both the highest peak, Mount San Gorgonio (or what used to be called Old Grayback), at 11,489 feet, and Big Falls, the highest waterfall in Southern California, at an elevation of 6,224 feet.[3] Mill Creek Canyon is also sometimes called the Valley of Falls for the many waterfalls along its length. Indeed, two of the most defining characteristics of the canyon, and of life in it, are its waters and recurring disasters. The valley itself is the Mill Creek Fault, an earthquake fault line at the easternmost tributary of the Yucaipa quadrangle of the notorious San Andreas Fault.[4] During storms, waters race down the steep mountainsides with debris flows of rock, mud and trees; cataclysmic floods have shaped and reshaped the canyon throughout time. Moreover, threats of fire and, at times, the folly of visitors pose additional challenges. The reality of only one way in and one way out brings into sharp focus both the remote uniqueness and the vulnerability of life in the two Mill Creek Canyon villages of Mountain Home and Forest Falls. These realities necessarily draw the canyon's residents into close community.

Mill Creek Road, circa 1900. *Courtesy Janice Gillmore private collection.*

A signature of this small valley is that it has often been a place of firsts in California history and, in one notable case, the history of the world. During the days of Spanish and early Mexican rule, people didn't often stray from the coasts, and ships were built mostly out of salvaged wrecks.[5] Although Mill Creek Canyon is about seventy miles inland, good timber was more easily accessible there and at a lower elevation than in the mountain ranges closer to the pueblo of Los Angeles. In 1832, American fur trapper William Wolfskill built *El Refugio*, the first schooner crafted from virgin timber to sail the West Coast.[6] That lumber was cut and hauled from Mill Creek Canyon.* The first sawmill in Southern California was built by French Angeleno Jean Louis Vignes and his nephew Pierre Sainsevain between 1841 and 1843. It was located at the mouth of Mill Creek Canyon and supplied oak casks for Vignes's El Aliso winery at the

---

* *El Refugio* is sometimes confused with the *Guadalupe*, a schooner built around the same time by shipwright Joseph Chapman in San Pedro. Wolfskill's *Refugio* was used for otter hunting briefly, then he sold it in San Francisco to Captain W.S. Hinckley. According to Hinckley's correspondence between 1832 and 1839, he sailed it to the Sandwich Islands and it never returned. *Guadalupe*, however, remained in California.

The Falls,
circa 1900.
*Courtesy Janice
Gillmore private
collection.*

Mill Creek Canyon in the San Bernardino Mountains, 2019. *Courtesy Marc Lester private collection.*

December 1966 flood in Mill Creek Canyon. *Courtesy Fred J. Beck Collection, California Department of Transportation Library.*

pueblo of Los Angeles.[7] At the end of the Mexican-American War in July 1847, a detachment of soldiers was sent out from Fort Moore in Los Angeles to Mill Creek Canyon to cut two trees that would be fashioned into a flagpole. My great-great-grandfather Philander Colton and his son Charles Edwin Colton were among them.[8] On July 4, 1847, the American flag was officially raised over Southern California for the first time on that flagpole.[9] Unquestionably, the most famous and far-reaching innovation in the canyon's history, however, was the first commercial transmission of three-phase AC power in the world, which was generated by Mill Creek.[10] AC current at present continues to power much of our world.

William Wolfskill, 1831. *Courtesy California Historical Society Collection, University of Southern California.*

Far from being a comprehensive narrative of Mill Creek Canyon's history and of all the people who have lived there, this book is a glimpse into the early days of the canyon before Americans found their way to Mill Creek and after they placed their stories on the land. Any errors, omissions or unwitting confabulations are mine. I know that you will keep me honest, and I hope that any new or different light on the subject will, over time, serve to advance our understanding.

Finally, history is a living thing that emerges, changes and grows over time. The act of writing about the past is haunted by lives undocumented, the silence of disenfranchised voices and things unseen while looking the other way. I have endeavored to be accurate, to use primary or contemporary sources and to find truth where it could be discovered. To my readers, I offer the clues along my path to follow for those who so desire, because history belongs to all of us, and the more it is shared, the greater is our knowledge.

Now, as we begin our journey into Mill Creek's fascinating history, the words of anonymous travelers in the 1890s set the scene for us:

The Santa Fe train rolled into the Redlands depot at 9:25, a fine canopy-topped carriage stood at the platform and the party rode off. It was a beautiful drive of about two hours through the orange groves and orchards bordering the city limits along the zanja to Crafton and Mentone.[11] After a pleasant

Forest Home stage, circa 1890s. Thomas Akers and Richard Jackson standing far right. *Courtesy Archives, A.K. Smiley Public Library.*

afternoon and delightful evening spent at the lovely Crafton Retreat; an hour's drive brought us to the mouth of the cañon. We gave a last backward glance over the San Bernardino Valley and mentally bade good-bye to our distant home and civilization for a fortnight. On, over the noisy, rocky Mill Creek; soon we see perched on the rugged face of a mountain a few hemlock trees which we hail with pleasure for we begin to realize we are nearing the mountains. The route is along the rugged Mill Creek cañon, enlivened by a refreshing breeze of cool mountain air direct from the peaks of Old Grayback. The road crosses and re-crosses the pure, clear, cold and swift stream perhaps a dozen times after entering the canyon. Immense boulders on either side mark the force of the current that has for ages washed them from their mountain fastnesses and deposited them, polished and sun-stained, in the valley below. Great cliffs of overhanging rocks stand out on either side in all their rugged grandeur, and high above, on the projecting shelves of stone, is seen an old derrick which remains as a silent sentinel to mark the spot where the immense building stones of the San Bernardino county courthouse were quarried out of the mountain. At 10:30 o'clock we reach our stopping place for the day and night, at an elevation of 3,300 feet.[12]

Come along, and let's begin.

THE FIRST PEOPLE OF MILL CREEK CANYON

Tribe after tribe it drew to the sacred portals. Carried down through a weary length of years! To this hour cherished by many a dark-skinned child of the mountains! Never, perchance, inscribed on parchment—yet written indelibly upon the Indian's heart!
—*Benjamin D. Wilson,* The Indians of Southern California in 1852

A.D. 20—For two thousand years, the Indigenous peoples of the area came to hunt and gather acorns and pine nuts in Mill Creek Canyon during the spring and summer months.

The history of the first people who traveled and stayed in Mill Creek Canyon is so ancient that their songs recall a time when Mount San Gorgonio smoldered as an active volcano. These first people are not just a historical people, a quaint artifact from a different time. Their descendants continue to live in Highland at San Manuel and the Banning area at Morongo. Even so, their culture and populations were severely disrupted, and the voices that knew the songs and stories about Mill Creek Canyon were all but silenced before the twentieth century.

Like shards of pottery, we have fragments of memory; some are the witness perspectives of those who came into contact with the *Yuhaaviatam,* or People of the Pines, and some are Indigenous, passed from mouth to ear. Few specific stories survive. According to contemporary understanding of traditional Cahuilla and Serrano lands, Mill Creek Canyon was a borderland between the two but generally agreed to be within the territory of the Yuhaaviatam and *Maarenga'yam* people, both known as Serrano. The famed Yuhaaviatam *ki'ika*, or chief, Santos Manuel, who saved his people from extinction, referred to Mill Creek Canyon as his country.[13] He also noted that it was the *Yucaiviatam* from *Yukaipat*, or what is now known as the Yucaipa Valley, who used the ancient trail up the canyon to gather pine nuts and acorns each year.

Living in Mill Creek Canyon was seasonal for the first inhabitants of the area, just as later it came to be a place for summer resorts. The Yuhaaviatam had no reason to stay year-round when they could easily walk to their more permanent village sites in the warmer valleys below rather than live in inclement conditions in the higher elevations.[14] The closest Serrano groups living near the canyon included a village identified with *tukut*, the wildcat, in the present-day Greenspot area; the Yucaiviatam of Yucaipa; and the *Wa'atcavitum* of *Wa'atcavit* in the present-day Redlands area. Both of the latter were identified as *wahil*, or coyote clan villages.[15] The clan system was important to regulate marriage, and a person always married outside his or her own clan, thus ensuring healthy bloodlines.[16] According to ethnographers, the Shoshonean ancestors of these people came to the area through a long migration by both land and sea about two thousand years ago.[17] They spoke an Uto-Aztecan *Takic* language and lived in small clan groups of twenty or so families, except at the Yucaipa and Morongo Valleys, where space and resources sustained larger villages. Typically, their dwelling places were near water sources, usually at the entrance to canyons. They spent the winters in the warmer valleys and the springs and summers in the higher elevations, such as in Mill Creek Canyon, gathering plants and hunting and fishing until the autumn months. A staple of their diet was acorns, which they made into a kind of porridge called *wiich* or into a flat bread similar to a tortilla. In the autumn, when the acorns were ripe, males, both children and adults, climbed high into the branches of the oak trees to shake the nuts down, and the women gathered them in baskets. They were then taken to the valley and stored in tule granaries.[18] There is evidence at some sites in the canyon of ground stones, where acorns may have been ground into flour.[19] Santos Manuel remarked that they hunted with bows and arrows and that they were a peaceable people who never engaged in intertribal wars like the Yuma, Chemehuevi, Mojaves and Pauites in the deserts to the east and south.

Traditional Serrano
kiich, circa 1900.
*Courtesy Banning
Library District.*

The tide-like rhythm of moving with the seasons was more or less uninterrupted, except perhaps by natural phenomena and local politics, for at least two thousand years. That tide changed when the first Europeans came into their territory in the eighteenth century. Although the songs of the Yuhaaviatam foretold the arrival of these people,[20] it signaled an end to the existence they had known for millennia.

Santos Manuel told this story in 1918, when he was thought to be over ninety years old.

> *The viruelas* [smallpox] *came three times and killed all the Serranos. The people tried to run away but died on the road and the coyotes ate them—men, women and children. But Manuel and family salieron muy bien* [they went very well]. *Manuel's friends would avisar* [warn] *him and say: "Tu puedes llevar los muchachos par la sierra,"* [You should take the children to the mountains] *and he took his family up here to kutáina't and none of them took the smallpox—once they stayed at kutáina't two months because of the smallpox epidemic down below. And also they went away to "el otro lado, Maronga mas paca"* [the other side of Morongo]. *And thus they escaped. Before these epidemics, the Serranos were very numerous and camped all over this country, e.g. remaining a while in kutáina't, then going to jukai'p'at* [Yucaipa] *for a little while. They ate game and bellota* [acorns].

Diseases and displacement to Mission San Gabriel Arcangel in the early 1800s were the first disruptions introduced by the Spaniards, and both would destroy large numbers of Serrano populations as well as traditional

Santos Manuel, age ninety. *Courtesy San Diego History Center.*

culture long before Santos Manuel was born.[21] Americans followed in the mid-nineteenth century.

One of the first Americans to interact routinely with the Indigenous populations in or near Mill Creek Canyon was pioneer Daniel Sexton from Louisiana, who arrived in Southern California with the Rowland-Workman Party in November 1841.[22] Working for Colonel Isaac Williams on the Chino Rancho, Sexton almost immediately came to cut timber in Mill Creek Canyon on the advice of the local Indigenous people.[23] He spent 1841 and 1842 timbering in the area, and his description of the canyon as he first experienced it offers a vague but tantalizing peek into Indigenous life along Mill Creek and in Redlands.

> *They cultivated and had their village on the southwest side of the ditch* [the Mill Creek zanja]*, and they cultivated on the north side.* [T]*he Indians had some tule houses, and some of the Indians lived in that building* [the Asistencia]*. The Indians told me those buildings were burned up in 1832; they killed about 500 Indians there; that was the Mission ranch building. I think* [Mill Creek water] *has been used there since the hills were made there. I don't know, but I expect Indians have lived there since Indians have lived anywhere, and they have always had water out of that creek. The Indians used to live near the Old San Bernardino mountain in olden times but there were a great many* [grizzly] *bears, and they were afraid of the bears...afraid to go into the brush in the canyon; if you were to see as many bears as I have seen there—why, I have seen the Yucipa* [sic] *full of them. I saw fifty bears at the least calculation around a cherry bush up in the side of the canyon.*

Bears feature prominently in both the history of Mill Creek Canyon and the culture of the Serrano people. Grizzlies were, unquestionably, fearsome animals, but what Sexton perceived as fear among the Indigenous people may also have been a deep respect. The Serrano had a special relationship with bears and didn't hunt or eat them, believing that the spirits of their ancestors inhabited the animals.

In the winter of 1875, George Weeks, a twenty-four-year-old journalist from New York who had contracted tuberculosis, agreed to go to Crafton, California, to take the cure at the sanitarium there. After a few nights of lying awake listening to the painful, wracking coughs of his fellow "one-lungers," as he referred to himself, he struck off on his own and met a rancher, "the Boss," who hired him as a ranch hand and gave him a place to live. Young

George also befriended the local people. Another perspective about bears was reflected in the beliefs of "Capitan Juan," who may have been Captain John Morongo. Weeks related the following:

> *One day in the fall I went down there* [the nearby rancheria or village] *with the Boss to see the Chief, Capitan Juan, in order to induce him to accompany us into the mountains to gather up the cattle which ranged there during the summer months, and drive them down into the valley for the winter. Juan agreed to go for the standard wage of a dollar a day. But as we were leaving, the Boss said to him in a joking manner:*
>
> *"I am going to take my new rifle, Juan, and perhaps we may see a bear and shoot—"*
>
> *That was as far as he got. Juan threw up his hands in dismay and with an expression of great apprehension on his countenance said:*
>
> *"Stop, Señor! Stop, Señor!"*
>
> *"Why should I stop?" asked the Boss, though he was well aware of the reason.*
>
> *"The bear will hear you!" said Juan. "I think he has already heard you! No, Señor, I will not go with you as I promised, for you will surely have trouble with the bear!"*
>
> *Nor could any amount of persuasion, even the offer of a higher rate of payment than at first agreed upon, induce him to relent. He simply but firmly would not go! The bear had undoubtedly heard the threat to shoot him, and would be sure to revenge himself upon any one who uttered that threat.*[24]

Sure enough, after the cattlemen had ridden partway up Mill Creek Canyon, they encountered a grizzly gorging on a steer that it had just killed. The bear, angered by the interruption, pursued the Boss and his horse, forcing the rancher to jump a precipitous ravine, narrowly escaping the grizzly's claws. When they saw Capitan Juan again a few days later, he said: "What did I tell you? I told you the bear would hear you if you said you were going to try to shoot him, and that he would take revenge and try to kill you. And he did hear you, and he did try to kill you! You yourself have said it!"

George Weeks concluded that Juan believed in an omniscient "Bear God," which was off the mark, but the relationship of both fear and respect for the grizzlies was well understood. Bears also figure in one of the few known Yuhaaviatam place-names in Mill Creek Canyon: *Hírnaqt fami,* or Bear

Left: Captain John Morongo. *Courtesy William H. Weinland Collection, the Huntington Library, San Marino, California.*

Right: Ethnographer John Peabody Harrington, circa 1920. *Courtesy California State University, Chico, Meriam Library Special Collections, Northeastern California Historical Photograph Collection.*

Shaman Rock, a very large stone near present-day Mountain Home Village at Thurman Flats. Santos Manuel related the legend of the remarkable land feature to J.P. Harrington.

> *They said that there was a bear that lived up in those two* [Strawberry Creek and City Creek] *canyons, and also frequented the ridge above where they joined, that kept killing people when they were on their road to the pinyons passing through those canyons. It was not a bear, they said, but a person* [a shaman who could turn himself into a bear]. *At last a man like informant is, a hunter, went up from Arrowhead Spring up that right-hand canyon and placed himself in the monte there and as that bear came past, he shot him from the side and the arrow went through his chest and out the other side. The bear, in great pain so that he did not recognize which was his home (aki), ran wounded way over to ani'tsip't (which is informant's country* [Mill Creek Canyon region]*). The bear died there and turned to a black rock with its head pointing Needles-ward* [east].[25]

Above: Bear Shaman Rock in the middle foreground. *Courtesy John D. Goodman II, private collection.*

Left: The head of a bear is discernible at the top left of Bear Shaman Rock. *Courtesy John D. Goodman II, private collection.*

James Ramos also noted that Yuhaaviatam stories say the bear was trying to reach the village on the other side of Yucaipa Ridge, where the bear shaman people lived.[26]

Santos Manuel and the other men who joined him and J.P. Harrington on their travels through the San Bernardino Mountains sometimes said that certain places were magic, areas of Mill Creek Canyon among them. Even today, it is said that the *pahas* or ceremonial leaders among the valley groups came to sing and pray in the canyon before the bighorn sheep hunts and that it was thought to be a place of special significance.

The history and teachings of the Serrano people were recorded in songs learned and memorized then passed from generation to generation across a nearly incomprehensible expanse of time. In these songs, it is said that their first ancestors came like smoke or mist or birds from the sky fleeing another world that could no longer sustain them.[27] Serrano elder Dorothy Ramon related this story.

> *Indians apparently used to live somewhere else. They were living on some planet similar to this one. The Serrano Indians came to a new world. There were apparently too many people living on the old planet. They were killing each other due to overpopulation. They did not get along. Their Lord brought them to a new world.*

The place they reportedly came to, which they call *Maara'*, is present-day Twentynine Palms, California. From the oasis of Maara', the ancestors of the Serrano spread west into the San Bernardino Mountains.[28] Their songs told them that a younger brother would come—a younger brother who had a choice. If this younger brother chose to do harm, it was said, he would lose his soul. Dorothy Ramon related: "Long ago they had a Lord. He told the Serrano people about the arrival of the white people....He told the Indians that he was going to bring His children (the white people) to this world. They (white people) were reportedly going to clothe us. The white people were going to tell us Indians things." This is what their songs told them long before their first encounters with Europeans.

After statehood in 1850, California's first governor declared on January 7, 1851, "that a war of extermination will continue to be waged between the two races until the Indian race becomes extinct."[29] In this environment, and with the discovery of gold in Holcomb Valley in the mountains as well as a series of incidents with wrongdoing on both sides of the equation, relations between the settlers in the San Bernardino Valley and the region's

Chief Genazio Cabezon and his captains, Charles C. Pierce, 1891. *Courtesy C.C. Pierce Collection, the Huntington Library, San Marino, California.*

Indigenous people became increasingly tense. On August 18, 1866, the *Wilmington Journal* in Los Angeles reported that a group of Chemehuevi Indians had shot a Dr. Smith in his bed in the San Gorgonio Pass. The assertion that "a military camp is very much needed in the neighborhood of San Bernardino to keep these Indians at a safe distance"[30] demonstrates the prevailing attitude of perceived threat. The settlers made no distinctions among tribal nations, and their fear was generalized across all Indigenous people. It erupted into a thirty-two-day campaign by the San Bernardino militia to seek out Indians in the mountains and exterminate them. While it is possible that some of this crusade took place in Mill Creek Canyon, specific incidents are undocumented. Ultimately, Santos Manuel was able to save fewer than thirty of his people by the end of this war in 1867.[31]

The people who had walked the trail up into Mill Creek Canyon to gather life-giving sustenance for millennia and whose territory had stretched from the sea to the Colorado River were rounded up and placed on small reservations by 1891.[32] They no longer came as villages to gather food along Mill Creek. Yet, the mountains, *'Aya' Qaych* (Mount San Gorgonio) and *Tarahiak* (Mount San Bernardino), and the place of pretty rocks high in the canyon called *Piá'kwa'jt*, as well as *Hírnaqt fami*, the Bear Shaman Rock, still bear witness to their long, long history on that land, which remains Yuhaaviatam traditional territory.

2

DANIEL SEXTON

AN ADVENTURER IN THE NEW WEST

If any young man is about to commence the world, we say to him,
publicly and privately, Go to the West.
—*Horace Greeley*

1841—Daniel Sexton was the first American resident in Mill Creek Canyon and partnered in the first sawmill in the San Bernardino Mountains, which gave the canyon and its creek their names.

D aniel Sexton was born in Concordia Parish, Louisiana, on March 23, 1818, to Daniel Sexton of Frederick, Maryland, and Ann Lewis of Virginia, the last born of their eight sons.[33] The Sextons had an indigo farm in Louisiana before moving northward along the Mississippi and settling at its confluence with the Arkansas River in Desha County, Arkansas, around 1830.[34]

In Sexton's early life, Arkansas was the frontier, pressing against Mexico, Texas and Indian Territory, which would become the state of Oklahoma.[35] In fact, the infamous Trail of Tears passed very near where he lived as a young man. On the other side of the frontier was the tantalizing prospect of the Pacific Ocean. In June 1841, the editor of the *Arkansas Times & Advocate* received a letter from Sexton, a twenty-three-year-old carpenter, saying he was departing with an exploring expedition to California from Sapling

Grove, Missouri. The company of 125 young men and about a dozen families intended to cross the Rocky Mountains together, then split into two companies, one bound for Oregon and the other for California.[36] Sexton was describing the famed Bidwell-Bartleson Party, the first company of overland American migrants to reach the West Coast.[37] Although Daniel did depart with that wagon train, he and some of his companions detoured via the Santa Fe Trail to New Mexico. There, he joined the Rowland-Workman Party, another group bound for the West Coast via the Old Spanish Trail. Daniel claimed he knocked an Indian down with his fists, which started a fight that encouraged the swift departure of Rowland and Workman,[38] two entrepreneurs and former trappers, both naturalized Mexican citizens. However, the two leaders of the party had reason enough of their own to get out of town, as they'd run afoul of Governor Manuel Armijo following a rebellion in Taos. After two months and a 1,200-mile journey that took them through the Cajon Pass and the San Bernardino Valley, they arrived at Mission San Gabriel on November 5, 1841. This was just four days after the Bidwell-Bartleson Party reached Northern California.

Daniel was in the foreign territory of Mexico, and only Mexican nationals could own land under law, which put him at a disadvantage. Moreover, he soon learned that navigating another country without identifying papers was problematic. Sexton wrote to his father in Arkansas, asking him to apply for a U.S. passport on his behalf. That passport application offers us our only portrait of Daniel Sexton.[39]

> *He was twenty-five years of age on March 23, 1843, was about five feet, nine or ten inches in height, square built, with broad shoulders on a large and powerful frame. His hair was of a light brown color inclining to sandy; eyes, between blue and hazel, more decidedly hazel; nose, straight and of an ordinary size; mouth, large; complexion, ruddy, light and sandy. He had a small scar on the left cheekbone just a little distance under the eye. This scar, while not large, was easily perceived, being of a deep red color. It was occasioned by a kick from a horse which had thrown him. Sexton's forehead was broad and high; his chin was neither long nor receding.[40]*

Daniel wasted no time putting his carpentry skills to use for Colonel Isaac Williams at Rancho Santa Ana del Chino, constructing ranch buildings. He remarked that when he arrived in the San Bernardino Valley, the whole country was then solely occupied by Indians and that Cahuilla chief Juan Antonio gave him permission to travel and log in his territory.[41] Sexton spent

Above: Arkansas frontier in 1839. *David H. Burr, cartographer. Library of Congress.*

Right: John Rowland, circa 1860. *Courtesy the Homestead Museum Collection.*

William Workman
with daughter
Antonia Margarita
Workman de
Temple, circa
1852. *Courtesy the
Homestead Museum
Collection.*

his first two winters logging in and around Mill Creek Canyon, Oak Glen
and the San Gorgonio Pass areas.

Sexton's relationships with Indigenous people were defining; he would
live with and advocate for them throughout his life.[42] He had an especially
close relationship with Chief Solano, who is credited with supervising
the building of the Mill Creek *zanja*. The old chief told Daniel stories
about a secret mine where the stones had magical and healing properties.[43]
Intrigued, Sexton wanted to know where the mine was located, but Solano
guarded the knowledge. "The chief said that if [Daniel] should marry
into his family, he knew that his children would be protected from the
encroachment of the Whites."[44] Solano offered his niece, Pacifica, but
twenty-four-year-old Daniel declined.

Three years into Sexton's sojourn in Mexican California, unrest
broke out among the *Californios* against unpopular Governor Manuel

Micheltorena.[45] The small community of Americans in Southern California banded together to protect themselves, and Sexton joined their company. Two years later, in 1846, California became embroiled in the Mexican-American War. According to accounts, twenty-seven-year-old Daniel was right in the thick of it under the command of Stephen W. Kearny. Most notably, Commodore Robert Stockton, who commanded the U.S. forces on both land and sea, tasked Sexton with the highly dangerous assignment of finding General John C. Frémont and delivering dispatches to him.[46] Throughout the Southern California campaigns, Sexton fought boldly with his American compatriots and was a survivor of the bloody Battle of San Pasqual in December 1846, among others.

After the war, Daniel acceded to Chief Solano's wishes and married Serena Pacifica Damian, known as Pacifica, in 1847. She was a mantua maker and needle worker and was considered one of the belles of Los Angeles.[47] Sexton soon returned to lumber work, which would, again, take him to Mill Creek Canyon and a partnership with a very influential Angeleno.[48]

Jean Louis Vignes, a French vintner who owned El Aliso Winery in the pueblo of Los Angeles, established the sawmill that gave Mill Creek and the canyon their names.[49] The sawmill was an enterprise for Vignes's nephew Pierre "Pedro" Sansevain, recently arrived from France, to mill wine casks out of the abundant oak available in the canyon.[50] To modern sensibilities, the idea that the closest mill to Los Angeles was more than seventy miles away in Mill Creek Canyon seems odd. But the vast semi-desert inland valleys had few trees, and the canyon had abundant timber with easier access than the San Gabriel or coastal ranges.[51] However, as Vignes described in a request to the governor in 1843, building the first mill was not without challenges.

On the 30th November, 1841, the Government Department granted permission for three years to the citizen Juan Ramirez to cut wood at San Bernardino, and for that purpose there was legally formed a company composed of the proprietor thereof, Pedro Sansevain and myself. In effect it was thus done and begun at the date when permission was given, incurring on my part all the expenses necessary for the undertaking of the opening of roads, transportation of machinery etc. Nearly two years after the establishment had been made it did not pay costs, nevertheless, making further expenses it was at last put in running order; but unfortunately, when we expected to gather the fruits of so much labor, a heavy squall upset the machinery, overthrowing it from its place, and leaving it covered

Jean Louis Vignes. *Courtesy Special Collections, Charles E. Young Research Library, UCLA.*

with the timber which had been cut. The large quantity of stones, mud and other rubbish cast by the storm, gives no hope of its being soon refitted, wherefore the partners, convinced of this fact, have separated and ceded their rights in my favor.[52]

By 1847, Pierre Sainsevain had acquired land in Santa Cruz and Vignes was elderly and ailing.[53] Vignes took Sexton as his partner to oversee the operation of the mill. In 1852, Sexton took ownership, but the enterprise lasted only two years, then Daniel sold to his former employer, Isaac Williams, on November 2, 1854.

Daniel and Pacifica moved to San Gabriel, and their family burgeoned to nine children into the next decade. Chief Solano and his wife, Coleta, lived with the Sextons at their new home. On his deathbed, Solano finally revealed the location of the secret mine. The "magical" ore proved to be tin at the Temescal Tin Mines, the only known tin mines in the United States at that time.[54] Unfortunately, Sexton's privileged status as the lone

American inheritor of the secret of the mine was swiftly challenged. This was the era of land disputes among Mexican grants, inheritances and new deeds competing for the same parcels of land.[55] Sexton also sold off percentages of his claim, probably to keep his family afloat, and everyone involved with the mines became ensnared in lawsuits for decades. Daniel apparently didn't give up on the dream of riches, however.[56] "Sometime in 1859, Daniel Sexton, a veteran of the battles of San Bartolo and the Mesa, became possessed of the idea that gold was secreted in large sacks near the ruins of San Juan Capistrano; and getting permission, he burrowed so far beneath the house of a citizen that the latter, fearing his whole home was likely to cave in, frantically begged the gold-digger to desist. Sexton, in fact, came near digging his own grave instead of another's, and was for a while the good-natured butt of many a pun."[57]

Disappointed in his attempts to own and cultivate land or discover wealth, Sexton turned to inventing for several years, which included a peculiar combination birdcage and aquarium, a new type of quartz mill, a double-piston steam engine, an air exhauster for racking off wines and liquors and a new type of dripless and airtight tap for kegs. Despite his eccentricities,

Daniel Sexton's pioneer peers, Pioneer Park, San Bernardino. *San Bernardino Public Library collection.*

Left to right: Daniel Sexton's son, John; granddaughter Neola Palen; and Jacob Van Zandt Wyckoff, Neola's husband, 1908. *Courtesy Susan Wyckoff private collection.*

Sexton was well respected in Southern California. He served as a grand juror and a delegate to the county Democratic convention and was called to testify in the high-profile water case *Craig, Cave, et al. vs. Craft, et al.* Perhaps more important, though, he won the affection of many throughout his life.[58] Finally settling in Colton, California, in 1888, he was inducted by the San Bernardino Society of California Pioneers as a founding member,[59] and several times, friends publicly advocated for his accomplishments and made pleas on his behalf in the press as he aged.

On October 21, 1894, Pacifica Sexton, the wife who'd shared Daniel's adventures for forty-seven years, passed away, following their eldest son, Daniel, who had succumbed to cancer at the end of the previous year.[60] At the remarkable age of eighty, on May 5, 1899, the old pioneer's long adventure ended with pneumonia at his home in Colton.[61] All but four of his children had predeceased him.

DAVID FREDERICK AND MARY ANN WINNER

WHEN THE SAINTS CAME MARCHING IN

Pioneers may be picturesque figures, but they are often lonely ones.
—*Nancy Astor*

1853—Mormon settlers David Frederick and Mary Ann Winner were the first documented year-round American residents to live in Mill Creek Canyon and raise a family there.

During the first half of the 1800s, western New York State was called the "Burned-Over District."[62] Religious revivalism and social experimentation swept across it like a wildfire as New England's expanding populations overtook its wilderness. This period and place gave rise to the Spiritualist movement and the women's rights movement as well as social experiments ranging from the celibate Shakers to free-love communes. At the onset of this fervor, David Frederick was born in Minden, New York, in 1801.[63] In 1845, he became a follower of Joseph Smith's Latter-day Saints, a new religion also founded in western New York in 1830.[64]

Mary Ann Winner was seventeen in 1846 when Joseph Smith was assassinated and his successor, Brigham Young, wanted his ostracized followers out of the United States and into foreign territory. Young organized a first party of emigrants to travel by sea to California on the ship *Brooklyn*; Mary Ann, with her parents and 5 siblings, was among them.[65] On February 4, 1846, 230 Mormon emigrants and 12 non-

Mormon travelers, plus crew, departed on a twenty-four-thousand-mile journey, the first recorded voyage of women and children around Cape Horn.[66] Shortly after departing New York Harbor, a terrifying storm in the Atlantic blew up, and the captain, Abel Richardson, told the passengers to prepare to die. During the storm, the two milk cows they'd taken for the voyage were battered to death by the violent tossing of the ship. The passengers, tied into their bunks, became desperately seasick. By the time the storm subsided, they'd been blown off course nearly to the coast of Africa. When they reached Cape Horn, supplies and water were running low, and both scurvy and rats were rampant among the passengers. Desperately navigating north toward Valparaiso, Chile, to resupply, gale winds blew them into Antarctic waters, where they were becalmed, ice in the rigging, uncertain they would survive.

At the same time, President James Polk declared war on Mexico on April 25, 1846. Brigham Young thought that service to the United States by his people would demonstrate goodwill and provide much-needed paychecks that would enable the Saints to reach the Salt Lake Valley in Mexican territory.[67] In need of troops, President Polk agreed to enlist Mormon volunteers for one year of service. David Frederick was among those who volunteered.

Little more than two weeks later, on May 4, exactly three months after setting sail, the beleaguered ship *Brooklyn* came into a bay in the Juan Fernandez Islands off the coast of Chile (best known as the desert islands of Daniel Dafoe's *Robinson Crusoe*), and the passengers left the ship for the first time. After a respite and resupplying with fresh water, but little food, they sailed for the Sandwich Islands (Hawaii). Ten passengers, many of them infants, and one crew member had already died on the voyage.

As the Mormon Battalion mustered into the U.S. Army at Council Bluffs, Iowa, and departed for California, the *Brooklyn* entered San Francisco Bay on July 31, 1846, and an American man-o'-war, the *Portsmouth*, made swiftly for them. They were boarded by uniformed men, striking terror in the emigrants, who had endured so much. When the officers reached the deck, they announced, "Ladies and gentlemen, I have the honor to inform you that you are in the United States of America." After fleeing the United States for tens of thousands of miles, they were, again, in U.S. territory. Worse, they had expected to be reunited with the overland Morman migrants on their arrival but found themselves alone.[68]

The Mormon Battalion, made up of 500 men and approximately 30 women and 50 children, marched with the U.S. Army two thousand miles through seven states and into Mexico, arriving in San Diego on January 29, 1847. It was the longest infantry march in U.S. military history.[69] When they arrived, the war was all but over, and the Mormon Battalion didn't fight a single battle. Although David Frederick volunteered with the battalion, he became ill in New Mexico and recuperated in Pueblo, Colorado.[70]

The Mormon volunteers still had six months to serve, and on June 8, 1847, a detachment of thirty-one soldiers was sent to Mill Creek Canyon to cut a "liberty pole." Taking two government mule teams, they logged two trees from the canyon then stripped and spliced them together with rawhide to create a one-hundred-foot flagpole, which they carted back to the fort. The Stars and Stripes was officially raised on that flagpole at Fort Moore for the first time in Southern California. Shortly thereafter, on July 16, the men of the Mormon Battalion were honorably discharged.

After their discharge, most of the battalion members made their way to Salt Lake City, but Brigham Young wanted to establish a colony in Southern California under the leadership of Amasa Lyman and Charles Rich. A company of 437 colonists, David Frederick among them, departed

Flagpole at Fort Moore. *Courtesy Security Pacific National Bank Photo Collection, Los Angeles Public Library.*

for California on March 24, 1851. They had 150 wagons, 588 oxen, 336 cows, 107 horses and 50 mules, plus loose stock. The party was plagued by blizzards, hostilities and an almost deadly lack of water crossing the desert. They made camp in a sycamore grove near present Devore, the last wagon arriving on June 11.[71] David Frederick was fifty when he arrived in the San Bernardino Valley. He had already lived a life filled with heartaches, having buried two wives and three children and left behind three surviving daughters for other families to raise.[72]

Lyman and Rich purchased the thirty-five-thousand-acre San Bernardino Rancho from the Lugo family on September 22, 1851, with a down payment of $7,000. At first, the settlers used the old adobe buildings of the original San Gabriel Mission rancho and built some crude log cabins.[73] In November, a rumored uprising led by Cupeño chief Antonio Garra mobilized them to build an enclosed fortification in only twenty days. Although Garra was arrested and executed a month later,[74] the Mormons stayed in the fort for a year before expanding into individual home plots. Planting crops in a two-thousand-acre community field, they hoped to be able to sell the surplus to make the payments on the ranch. As they laid out the plan for their city and began to build, the need for lumber was foremost in their considerations.

Lyman and Rich formed a partnership with fellow settler Theodore Thorpe to build a sawmill in Mill Creek Canyon, farther east up-canyon from Sexton's. A road construction crew was sent out, but they quickly reported that building a road up the rocky wash would be impossible. Lyman and Rich insisted, and the road to the selected mill site was painstakingly constructed.

Lyman's personal journal entries offer glimpses into the building of the sawmill that summer.

> *July 15, 1853; Today made some ineffectual efforts to raise some help to work on the sawmill in the Mill Creek Kanyon.*
>
> *July 18, 1853; Monday. This morning Brother [George] Sirrine with five hands started for the Mill Creek sawmill.*
>
> *August 1, 1853; Monday. Went to the Saw mill on Mill Creek. Arrived at dark, found the men prospering in the work.*
>
> *August 2, 1853; Tuesday. Today tarried at the mill.*
>
> *August 4, 1853; Thursday. We started the mill. It worked well.*
>
> *August 5, 1853; Friday. We spent the morning in improving about the mill. Continued all day.[75]*

A short time later, some of the *Brooklyn* Saints from San Francisco decided to join the colonists in San Bernardino,[76] including the George Winner family with twenty-three-year-old daughter Mary Ann, who was unmarried and heavily pregnant when they arrived in 1853. Perhaps out of kindness and to legitimize her child, David Frederick, who was then fifty-one, married Mary Ann on October 16, 1853. She gave birth to a daughter, Georgiana, on December 3.

Lyman's journal on May 2, 1854, noted: "Tuesday. Today in company with Br[other]s Sidney Tanner & David Frederick went to Mill Creek Mill to see the condition of the mill and engaged br[other] Frederick to saw for $3.00 per thousand [board feet of milled lumber] and his wife to cook for the mill hands at one bit [12 and one-half cents] per hand per day and they have their provision funded."

Soon thereafter, the Fredericks moved to the sawmill and were tending to its operation, the hired hands and dozens of hogs. Sadly, little Georgiana passed away a month after they made Mill Creek Canyon their home.

Frederick maintained a loving correspondence with his daughters from his prior marriages. On January 20, 1855, he wrote to Mary Elizabeth, his second daughter, in Salt Lake. His exact wording is faithfully reproduced here.

> *Mar E my belove Daughter....I am tending a sawmill about twenty miles from the city for Bro. Lyman and Rich in Canion Call Mill Crick, a health place and pure water but rather lonsome plase but that matters not so that we are duing the will of him that has sent us....Mary Ann your stepmother wishes to see you and wants you come hear and live in San Barnideno wheare she may injoy yur society. We have a fine young son thirteen days, he waide nine pounds when he was born, he is well and Mary Ann is smart and up aboout the house....Perhapps you would like to knowe his name, is David Junior. When you receve this write againe, yors as ever./signed/ David Frederick*[77]

The lonesomeness of Mill Creek Canyon did wear on David and Mary Ann, and letters and journals speak of trips into San Bernardino as often as possible, with stays at Amasa Lyman's large home for a week or more at a time before returning to the mill, which was located near the present maintenance buildings at Forest Home.

During the building of the sawmill on Mill Creek, and later, Amasa Lyman secretly experimented with Spiritualism and automatic writing in seances held at the mill site, though it's not known whether the Fredericks

Left: Amasa Lyman Home, 1863. *Courtesy Bancroft Library, University of California, Berkeley.*

Below: David Ira Frederick, born in Mill Creek Canyon, and his wife, Sophia Degraw. *Courtesy David Degraw private collection.*

participated in them. A man named Calvin Reed took dictation for the spirit of Joseph Smith's brother Hiram, who had been Lyman's close friend. Ultimately, these covert activities carried out on Mill Creek would lead to Lyman's excommunication from the church.[78]

David and Mary Ann Frederick had two daughters while living in the canyon. Cynthia Julia was born in April 1856, and Martha Catherine was born in March 1858. They also had a son, David Ira. It's hard to know what the fate of the colony would have been had they been left to evolve, but on October 30, 1857, Brigham Young called the colonists back to help defend Salt Lake City against the U.S. Army in the short-lived Utah War.[79] The Fredericks didn't leave right away with the other members of the colony, probably because Mary Ann was heavily pregnant with Martha. David was also overseeing the sale of the sawmill, which finally sold on June 22, 1858, to the Bachman Mercantile Company of Los Angeles.[80]

Sadly, Mary Ann Winner Frederick's astonishing journey ended too soon the following year on February 12, 1859, when she died of tuberculosis at the age of thirty-one just after they reached Parowan, Utah. David was fifty-eight years old. He gave his daughters Cynthia and Martha to other families to raise and kept only his son, David, near. Despite a litany of ails in his pension application in 1880 as a veteran of the Mexican-American War when he was seventy-nine, David Frederick lived a long life, finally passing away at the age of eighty-eight in Huntington, Emery County, Utah.[81]

PETER FORSEE

FORSEEVILLE AND THE McHANEY GANG

Land lasts longer than blood or love.
—*Annick Smith,* Homestead

1869—The first named place in Mill Creek Canyon was Forseeville, the homestead of Peter Atticus Forsee, at the confluence of Mill Creek and Mountain Home Creek.

PETER FORSEE AND FORSEEVILLE

Peter Atticus Forsee was a Virginian born in Powhatan County on December 26, 1814.[82] His father, James, became a lawyer and migrated with his young family to Noblesville, Indiana, by 1830 to practice law.[83] In Indianapolis, young Peter studied law at Hanover College, Indiana's first private college, and learned the printing trade working for the *Indianapolis Journal* newspaper.[84] He practiced as a lawyer for a few years, and at the age of twenty-five in 1839, "he married a beautiful and accomplished wife and became the father of four children. Sadly, his wife [Ann Burk] died in 1848, his second daughter soon followed, and his youngest son died in 1849."[85] Peter left his surviving children, John and Amanda Jane, with their maternal grandparents and followed his parents and siblings to the gold fields of

California.[86] The Forsee family arrived in Placerville, El Dorado County, on September 17, 1850, though Peter left them and struck out on his own to Coloma.[87] Forsee's pioneer peers gave an account of his accomplishments in the San Bernardino *Daily Courier* in 1888.

> *He tried mining for some time but preferred the excitement of the hunter, and during two years he hunted for the San Francisco markets and the northern mines, and during these two years he killed twenty-two grizzlies, forty-three black and cinnamon bear and one hundred and seventy deer, and was known as the champion hunter.*[88]

Peter was thirty-six, a restless, unsettled man moving around the gold country in Northern California and Nevada in the 1850s and early 1860s,[89] farming or working as a printer or a lawman. Southern California was also unsettled, especially in the San Bernardino Valley. The departure of the majority of the Mormon colony left a void of governance, and a period of wild lawlessness ensued.[90] In the summer of 1860, gold was discovered in Holcomb Valley in the mountains, sparking a rush. Conflicts between the settlers and the Indigenous populations were a tinderbox.[91] The citizens of

Pioneer believed to be Peter Atticus Forsee. *Courtesy San Bernardino Pioneer and Historical Society.*

San Bernardino begged for the presence of the U.S. Army and its protections; a detachment was sent to establish Camp Carleton in August 1861.[92] Adding to this instability, a tide of emigrants flooded into California just as disaster struck in January 1862 with an unprecedented statewide flood. By the time the deluge ended, California was under water and vast lakes covered the inland valleys to the extent that parts of the state had to be navigated by steamboat.[93] Much of that torrent in Southern California descended through Mill Creek Canyon and the Santa Ana River drainage, wiping out the few settlements in its path as it rushed violently toward the sea.[94] Livestock and houses were destroyed in the San Bernardino Valley, Camp Carleton was displaced, the Mill

Creek mills were swept away and debris clogged the mouth of Mill Creek Canyon, making it impassable for some time.

Just as the area was beginning to recover, the outbreak of the Civil War caused new migrants from both North and South to become divided and suspicious. In one official report about San Bernardino, it was noted, "This place was the hot-bed of secessionism in California."[95] Tensions were high, and lines were quickly drawn. Edwin A. Sherman, the rabble-rousing editor of the Unionist *Weekly Patriot*, wrote: "Secret meetings continue to be held all over this lower country, and secession and disunion is boldly avowed in our streets. Shooting continues to be the order of the day, and drunken desperadoes and Southern cutthroats damn the Stars and Stripes and endeavor to create disturbances all of the time."[96]

The overwrought reports of the day seemed to find Southern sympathizers lurking behind every tree. Many people erroneously believe that Mill Creek Canyon was a haven for Confederate sympathizers and the scene of Civil War battles. However, there are only two officially documented instances of secessionist activity in the canyon. On May 13, 1863, a doctor named Dickey reported to Major Clarence Bennett that his spy, Johnny McGaw, found four men in a "secessionist camp" in Mill Creek Canyon. The men told McGaw they were working a quartz vein, but he didn't believe them. Bennett's subsequent report to Lieutenant Colonel R.C. Drum on May 25, 1863, also noted that "signal fires have been kept burning nightly on the high peak of the mountains near the head of Mill Creek." What the fires really meant, no one was certain. Nevertheless, the farthest western battle of the Civil War was, in fact, fought at Picacho Pass, northwest of Tucson, Arizona, on April 15, 1862,[97] nowhere near Mill Creek Canyon.

In the wake of all of that tumult, Peter Forsee arrived in San Bernardino in 1867 at the age of fifty-three with his elderly father and some siblings.[98] He had been a deputy sheriff in Ukiah, Mendocino County, and dealt with North/South tensions and lawlessness there. Earlier that year, he had written and published a memoir titled *Five Years of Crime in California*. The memoir detailed the murder spree of G.W. Strong, who was executed at the age of twenty-three in Ukiah City on August 31, 1866.[99] It seemed that Forsee's reputation as a lawman preceded him; a short time after arriving in San Bernardino, Forsee and Nicholas Earp, father of the famous Earp brothers, stood against an angry crowd intent on lynching a prisoner at the Colton jail. Despite his bravery, however, Forsee had likely seen enough violence as a lawman and apparently wanted a pastoral life.

Peter Forsee homestead. *Courtesy Janice Gillmore collection.*

Forsee and fellow pioneer William Petty, also from Mendocino County, where he'd worked as a lumberman, formed a partnership in the "Happy Home Ranch" and homesteaded at the confluence of Mill and Mountain Home Creeks around 1869.[100] They built a home and outbuildings, then planted three hundred fruit trees.[101] Although the occasional mountain man, prospector or hunter made a temporary home in the valley, Forsee and Petty had Mill Creek Canyon to themselves as the only year-round residents. That is, until Petty decided to take a wife in September 1875. Petty and Forsee dissolved their partnership. Forsee took the lower half and Petty the upper, to which he moved his wife and stepchildren after building them a home.

Forsee's ranch became known as the town of Forseeville, although it seems to have been more a playful designation than anything official.

Forseeville is booming. It is getting to be a city of the first importance— during the hot months. The city was divided into two wards at the beginning of the season, and the name of Forseeville and Peterson given to the different wards. Uncle Peter Forsee was elected Mayor, and R.H. Curtis and Stewart

Wall were elected Marshals. The citizens are an orderly and peaceable set as a rule, although sometimes at the approach of new-comers they greet them with yells that would shame an Apache warrior.[102]

Even though Forseeville never formally became a town, it was a busy summer destination, and "Uncle" Peter's hospitality and kindness were renowned.[103] When he went into the city, he gave children his apples and stopped off at the newspaper offices with gifts and stories.[104] Accounts about his life and pursuits in the mountains indicate that he was happy in Mill Creek Canyon hunting or fishing on Forsee Creek, where he secured fishing rights,[105] growing thirty varieties of award-winning apples, leading groups on adventures into the high country, or playing practical jokes, and leading hijinks while hosting visitors on his ranch.

In 1877, Peter's long-lost daughter, Amanda Jane, whom he'd left in Indiana, came to Forseeville with her son John Ball and second husband, Sylvanus Thurman, to visit her father.[106] Amanda and her husband liked it well enough to homestead their own land below Forsee's place. The following year, after living as a bachelor for almost three decades, Peter Forsee married again at the age of sixty-three on February 24, 1878.[107] His bride was Martha McHaney, a fifty-year-old widow from Missouri with five children. Peter brought his new family to live at his Mill Creek ranch.[108]

THE McHANEY GANG

As the 1880s dawned, people took note of a strange, though subtle, crime wave that crept into the San Bernardino area, especially around the mountains. Cattle disappeared, there were unexplained deaths, curious frauds and assaults were perpetrated, as well as robberies and arson. One has to wonder how long it took Peter Forsee, a man of the law, to realize that his two eldest stepsons, William McHaney, twenty-one, and James McHaney, eighteen, were outlaws. The boys' activities were covered by Bill's work with his stepfather as a fruit farmer and Jim working a series of jobs for short periods of time, including guiding in the mountains and working on the Big Bear Dam. As the end of the decade approached, all did not seem well in Peter Forsee's marriage to Martha McHaney, and he spent increasing amounts of time in the city, then went to live with his sister Martha Van Tassell in El Monte as his health began to fail. Beloved "Uncle" Peter passed away on November 24, 1888, at his sister's home. On December 28, his peers in the San Bernardino Society of California Pioneers lauded him, remarking on his love for his home in Mill Creek Canyon.

Forsee made his will little more than a month before he died. In it, he made no mention of his wife, Martha, and left his entire estate to his son John B. Forsee in Missouri.[109] Notably, he also specified that he gave nothing to his daughter Amanda Jane Thurman.[110] John refused Peter's estate, and the court awarded the ranch and all of Peter's worldly goods, which amounted to a value of $13,500, to Martha in 1889.[111]

After their stepfather's death, Jim and Bill McHaney associated with other ne'er-do-wells, such as the thieving Chestnut brothers,[112] violent Button brothers and murderer Charley Marshall, as well as Charlie Martin. Martin, who had served five years in the state penitentiary for robbery, killed thirty-five-year-old miner Frank L. James[113] with the McHaneys but got off the murder charge by alleging self-defense. Ironically, Martin later became chief of police for the city of San Bernardino in June 1917.[114] The boys and these associates became known as the McHaney Gang.

Bill McHaney, considered the more likeable of the brothers, may have been a somewhat reluctant participant. The worst thing he was ever convicted of was trying to kiss an unwilling married lady, for which he had to pay a fifteen-dollar fine.[115] Jim McHaney was a much different story. In April 1892, he was arrested for cattle rustling after the remains of stolen cattle were found at his butcher shop in Banning.[116] He'd likely been getting away with it for several years, judging by the documented activities of his cohorts. Despite having been caught red-handed, Jim was acquitted.[117] He and the gang moved on to trying to poach on mining claims. In this endeavor, they finally hit it big through very bizarre circumstances.

As the story goes, an old prospector walked into Tingman's grocery store in Indio at the beginning of 1895 and told the grocer a wild tale about finding a canyon filled with gold bricks stamped with strange hieroglyphics and rocks veined with gold ore. The miner said that he found piles of human bones all around and at night the dead men rose up and chased him from the canyon with his haversacks filled with gold bars. The prospector showed Tingman some of the bars before selling him his mining equipment and boarding a train to Arizona. The next day, Tingman went to his partner in the Lost Horse Mine in the Morongo Mountains, where the McHaneys were hanging around, and told this strange story. Jim McHaney later claimed that he was looking for a place to water his livestock when his horse led him into a canyon with a large spring, where he discovered the mine. Whatever the circumstances, the McHaneys rushed to record the claim in both Riverside and San Bernardino Counties.[118] Their sister Carrie's husband, Harry Harrington, commented: "A million dollars for our claims would not be a temptation. Why, man, you can't conceive of the richness of the find until you see it. We have all the water we need, and the water belongs to us. The ore we have already crushed runs up in the thousands per ton, and it is only poor ore in comparison with what we have in sight. I am not an enthusiast, but I say to you the boys today have the richest claim ever discovered in California."[119]

The Desert Queen Mine, as they named their El Dorado, did pay out richly for a few years, and Jim became a swell, exhibiting his riches in a diamond-studded hatband and cane.[120] He wore suits and drank champagne and ensured that he would be able to tie one on whenever he wanted by buying the Klondike Saloon in San Bernardino.[121] His siblings Bill and Carrie began to worry about Jim's excesses. They tried to put someone in place to manage their wealth and restrain their brother, but Jim balked, enjoying the lifestyle too much.[122] By the turn of the century, the Desert Queen began to falter. Jim secretly used what ore he had to cover lead slugs and pass them off as five-dollar gold pieces through his saloon and the tamale stands in San Bernardino.[123] The gambit didn't work for long. On March 10, 1900, Jim McHaney was arrested for passing

Left: "Diamond" Jim McHaney. *Courtesy California State Archives.*

Right: "Jailbird" Jim McHaney. *Courtesy California State Archives.*

Bill McHaney. *Courtesy Joshua Tree National Park Museum Collections.*

counterfeit money and counterfeiting.[124] He was sentenced to three years in the San Quentin penitentiary.[125]

The McHaneys' mother, Martha Forsee, sold Forsee's Mill Creek ranch in June 1892 to longtime San Bernardino cattleman and entrepreneur George Tyler.[126] Martha and her eldest daughter, Augusta, lived comfortably in Banning until Martha's death on June 10, 1911, at the age of eighty-seven.[127] Jim served his time in San Quentin and later worked for the public utilities in Los Angeles. He died there in 1931.[128] Bill McHaney became a hermit, the first American settler to live at the oasis in Twentynine Palms, and he spent his life raising cattle and mining. In January 1937, Bill Keyes, a fellow pioneer rancher and miner, found Bill's remains in a cabin in Morongo Valley, where he'd died of pneumonia.[129]

WILLIAM PETTY AND ELIZABETH JACKSON

TRUE SETTLERS

Water is a pioneer which the settler follows, taking advantage of its improvements.
—*Henry David Thoreau*

1875—William Petty married widow Elizabeth Jackson, and their ranchland stretched from present-day Mountain Home Village to above the Mill Creek bridge, including Monkeyface Falls.

William Bailey Petty's trail to Mill Creek is familiar among pioneer narratives. He was born in Scioto, Pickaway County, Ohio, in 1817[130] while his parents, Absalom and Louisa, were on the move heading westward. They would go as far as Missouri before putting down any roots. William was still living with his parents in Pike County, Missouri, at the age of thirty-three when he caught gold fever and headed to the mining camps in Plumas County, California.[131] He was tall and sturdy by description,[132] undaunted by the hard work of mining. As many men found, though, riches weren't quite so easy to grasp as the news would have them believe, so Petty moved on, working as a lumberman in Calpella, Mendocino County.[133]

It seems likely that William Petty and Peter Forsee knew one another in Mendocino County, as the distance between Calpella and Ukiah is only about seven miles.[134] Regardless, they chose to form a partnership after both arrived in San Bernardino and selected Mill Creek Canyon as the site of their new home.[135] Forsee and Petty were squatters in Mill Creek Canyon.[136] That's not surprising, considering that Peter's father, Judge James Forsee, frequently sided with squatters in Sonoma County and was referred to as a "noisy squatter" himself while running for the senate there.[137] However, there were very practical reasons why they weren't able to claim the land legally. The first survey of the area following California statehood was in 1857, but it only mapped the mouth of the canyon and nothing inside its confines.[138] Without a survey, there wasn't an official mechanism for homesteading. A further complication arose when, in 1866 and 1871, the federal government gave one-mile-square sections of land (640 acres) to the Southern Pacific Railroad that alternated with one-mile-square sections of public lands.[139] As it happened, the land that Forsee and Petty chose became section 9 in the 1896 survey and was owned by the Southern Pacific Railroad.[140] Ownership would mean purchasing the land from the Southern Pacific, not homesteading it for free as public land.[141] Perhaps unaware of these complications, Forsee and Petty busily planted fruit trees (mostly peach and apple), acquired a stock of hogs and cattle and grew a large vegetable garden, including a big potato patch that Petty lovingly tended.[142] The arrangement seems to have been ideal for about five years, but into this bachelor Eden came a woman.

Elizabeth Archer Jackson was born in Schuyler County, Illinois, and her story was quite similar to William Petty's.[143] By 1850, the Archer family had made their way to Bates County, Missouri, where their neighbors were Zadock and Elizabeth Robertson Jackson and their four children.[144] Zadock Jackson had traveled the Northwest extensively, and he was hired on to guide a wagon train to Oregon.[145] Their neighbors the Archers were members of that party, too. According to a descendant, Zadock's wife died while they were on the trail, and seventeen-year-old Elizabeth Archer stepped in to care for the widower's children.[146] The party of settlers made it to Medford, Oregon, where Jackson stayed for some time before he decided to head south to California. It was there in Petaluma, Sonoma County, that Zadock Jackson and Elizabeth Archer were married on February 18, 1854.[147] The fate of Zadock's children with his first wife is difficult to discern, but he and Elizabeth started a family of their own. George Jackson was born in 1859, Mary Frances in 1865, Richard in 1867 and Lee in 1872. Zadock established the first commercial nursery in the state and became the road commissioner and then county supervisor for Sonoma's first district.[148] In 1860, he moved his family to San Bernardino, where he bought land between Tippecanoe and Waterman Avenues along

Left: Elizabeth Jackson Petty. *Courtesy Sandra Chase private collection.*

Right: George Jackson. *Courtesy Norma Harvey private collection.*

the Santa Ana River to pasture his mules. By 1870, they'd moved on to Prescott, Arizona, where Zadock's brother had discovered a gold mine.[149] After trying to promote and work the mine for three years, they failed, and the Jacksons returned to San Bernardino.

Zadock was building a diversion dam and a new nursery and needed lumber from the mountains. "While bringing a pack train loaded with lumber, he shot a deer for camp meat. He put the deer on the back of a gentle mule and started down the mountain. The mule was upset by the smell of blood from the deer and wouldn't cross the creek. He picked up a stick and walked around in back of the mule and hit her to make her cross the creek. The mule kicked Zadock in the stomach. He died a few days later at the home of Lewis Cram in East Highland, California on March 14, 1874."[150]

Elizabeth Jackson sold Zadock's estate to support herself and her children, but she was still in a very precarious position as a woman alone with a daughter and three sons, the youngest only three years old.[151] It's intriguing to imagine how Elizabeth Jackson and William Petty met, but that particular story remains uncertain. What is certain is that they married on September 5, 1875.[152] Two months later, Forsee and Petty called their partnership in their Mill Creek Canyon ranch quits. They agreed to split the property, placing a north/south dividing line in the middle, and Forsee gave Petty his choice of which half he wanted. Petty chose the upper half on the east side and claimed the right to half the apple crop for four years. They further agreed that when the time came for the government to survey the land, they would each claim only their part of the quarter section they felt they were entitled to by squatter's rights. It was an amicable separation, and they still shared water, taking turns irrigating their crops by agreeing on a time to divert water to their individual orchards and fields. A channel that Petty dug to develop water in a *cienega*, or wetland, on his upper half ran down to Forsee's house, and the two men built a flume to divert water from Mill Creek for irrigation. The neighborly feeling continued until Peter married Martha McHaney and she demanded household water.

In 1876, Forsee was supposed to guide a group of fourteen men from the Smithsonian Institution comprising botanists, entomologists and geologists as well as interested others to the top of old Mount San Bernardino.[153] For some reason, he was unable to do it. Instead, the group hired William Petty for ten dollars as their guide.[154] Truman Reeves, a Civil War veteran who had lost his arm in the Battle of Cold Harbor in Virginia in 1864, had relocated to San Bernardino for his health and opened a jewelry store. He was one of the organizers of the journey and, because there were a number of veterans in their party, was determined to make it a Memorial Day to remember. Everything went fine on the way up, and the group held a moving memorial service for their fallen comrades on the top of the peak above the clouds looking down on the San Bernardino Valley. On their way down, however, Petty's skill as a guide proved faulty. Reeves later chronicled the journey.

> *On our return trip to our camping place of the night before, about one half of the party, including the guide, started for camp by what [Petty] called the cut-off. It ran down the ridge, due south, from the top of the mountain. The descent was easy for a quarter of a mile, but finally we came to a jumping-off place, that looked to be several thousand feet to the bottom. So, the guide said, "We will go down into the canyon and over the ridge beyond." Now it must have been six hundred feet down a shale slide to the bottom of that canyon. As soon as we were on the shale rock it commenced to slide with us, and the farther we went the faster we went, with the shale*

A barn on the Jackson Ranch, 1918. *Courtesy Southern California Edison Collection.*

coming down upon us, cutting us badly. When we reached the bottom of that canyon, horror of horrors! we found the same old shale rock on the opposite side to climb up! Here we were engulfed in a canyon, whose sides were more difficult to climb than the pyramids of Egypt, and we could not follow the canyon down to the valley because of a very large waterfall that we could not get over or around. [Petty] said, "Boys, we are lost; but I know where my mule is; he's on yan ridge;" and he took his ax and gun and started up the canyon,—I suppose to the top of the mountain. The rest of us decided to elect Mr. D.W. Frazee, the editor of the San Bernardino Guardian, *as our guide and captain, he being the oldest; and we soon found that he was equal to the occasion, for we managed to climb the wall of the canyon in safety. Now, no well-equipped mountain party would think of taking a trip in the mountains without a bottle of what is often called "snake-bite remedy;" and we, of course, were well equipped. Well, when we got to the top of the ridge, we drank the contents of the bottle and made a record on the fly-leaf of a note-book something like the following: Lost on San Bernardino Mountain, May 30, 1876, the following persons. Then we signed our names, placed the paper in the bottle, corked it up tight and put it in a hollow tree. Many times, I have wondered if that bottle were ever discovered. In about three hours we made our way to the camp; and Petty, the guide, came in some time during the night, more dead than alive, leading his mule.* [155]

William Petty may have been lacking skills as a guide, but he was a good stepfather to Elizabeth's three boys, George, Richard and Lee Jackson. They all worked the ranch together, digging irrigation ditches, farming, fencing and taking care of the livestock and crops. It's hard to imagine now in the rocky, scrubby, dry moonscape that Mill Creek Canyon has become, but Petty describes fertile fields of wheat, barley and alfalfa on his land and wide swaths of crops, including potatoes, beans and artichokes. Sadly, however, all was not well on the Petty place, as it was known. In 1882, Petty sold all of his interest in the ranch to his wife, Elizabeth, and left for San Bernardino then went back to lumbering in the mountains.

In 1888, Petty's erstwhile partner, Peter Forsee, died, and the following year, Peter's widow, Martha McHaney Forsee, sold his ranch to George Tyler. The Tylers insisted that they had purchased water rights with their land from the Southern Pacific Railroad and that Elizabeth Jackson had no right to it for irrigation. [156] The Tylers sued Elizabeth Petty, and William returned in 1892 to testify on her behalf. Elizabeth prevailed in her fight for

George and Olive Jackson. *Courtesy Norma Harvey private collection.*

her right to the water on her land,[157] but somewhat ironically, she died of water-borne typhoid fever the following year on September 23, 1893, at the ranch in Mill Creek Canyon. She was fifty-nine years old. Petty went to Los Angeles, where he died of congestive heart failure two years later at the age of seventy-eight.[158]

At the time of Elizabeth Petty's death, her son George was a man of thirty-four with his own homestead in Mill Creek Canyon. He'd married a girl from nearby Yucaipa named Olive Clemence in 1886.[159] His brothers, however, were still young men. Richard was about twenty-five and not yet married; Lee was twenty-one. The death of Elizabeth Petty, their pioneering mother, meant that the brothers who had grown up free to roam in a wilderness would have to find their own ways in the canyon.

6

SYLVANUS THURMAN

TOURISM AND DONKEY TALES

*Thousands of tired, nerve-shaken, over-civilized people are beginning to find out
that going to the mountains is going home; that wildness is a necessity.*
—*John Muir,* Our National Parks

1882—Sylvanus Thurman was the first tour operator
in the San Bernardino Mountains. The Thurman Flats
Picnic Area near where his home once stood in Mill
Creek Canyon still bears his name.

The exceedingly tall, lanky Sylvanus Thurman would be the
quintessential picture of the pioneer outdoorsman except for one
quirk; he always wore a straw boater hat like those worn by members
of a barbershop quartet. Sylvanus was born in Taney County, Missouri,
on April 5, 1851, and his grandfather plied a flatboat on the Mississippi
River and fought in the Battle of New Orleans under Andrew Jackson.[160]
Sylvanus's father, Elisha Thurman, and mother, Eliza, farmed in the
Ozarks before loading their family into wagons pulled by oxen to make
a seven-month journey to the West Coast. Sylvanus "helped drive the ox-
teams and the cattle, taking his turn at standing guard, and early learning
the lessons of self-reliance and courage." The eldest of four siblings, he
had three brothers and a sister, and he was ten years old when they arrived
in Amador County, California, in 1860 to farm there. The family moved

north to Oregon for a few years then to the Los Angeles area, farming in La Puente and El Monte and finally settling near Downey.

As he came of age in the 1870s, Sylvanus made an early marriage to a young woman in San Bernardino named Charlotte Ann Allison when he was twenty-two.[161] It was short-lived, but it is his second marriage that is defining in our story. In 1878, Thurman married Amanda Forsee Ball, Peter Forsee's long-lost daughter from Indiana who was then Mrs. Amanda J. Ball,[162] five years older than Sylvanus and a mother to son John Ball. After their marriage, Thurman tried raising sheep and farming in El Monte and Verdugo but was severely hindered by a long period of drought. When those endeavors proved fruitless, he went to work for Springer and Van Tassel, running a freighting company out of Tombstone, Arizona. Van Tassel was Amanda's uncle, but that job also didn't last long.

According to Thurman, he had "known the Forsee place in Mill Creek Cañon since 1877 and…in '82 I lived on the Forsee place and farmed it."[163] Thurman worked Forsee's ranch first then claimed his own land just below

Sylvanus Thurman fishing on the Whitewater River. *Courtesy Archives, A.K. Smiley Public Library.*

that of his father-in-law. From his ranch, he began conducting burro pack trains into the mountains to Seven Oaks and Bear Valley.

Meanwhile, in 1877, entrepreneurs from the East, Edward G. Judson, a New York stockbroker, and Frank E. Brown, an engineer and surveyor, both bought land in the settlement of Lugonia, (named for the Lugo family, which had held the original land grant), located in the south end of the San Bernardino Valley. Identifying an opportunity in the excesses of fruit that year, they started a fruit-drying and -packing company. In 1881, Judson and Brown began buying up land for agricultural development and incorporated the Red Lands Colony. However, the nearby sources of water, such as Mill Creek and the Santa Ana River, were inconsistent, especially in the summer months, and they knew that if they were going to make a success of their venture, they would have to find or develop a year-round source of water for irrigation. Brown was actively seeking the answer to his water problem, traveling the mountains looking for a place to build a dam and reservoir to retain the ample winter water for use in the hot, arid summer months. Thurman and Jim McHaney were Brown's frequent companions on trips up to Seven Oaks on the Santa Ana River and beyond to Bear Valley.[164] When Brown commenced building the Bear Valley Dam in 1883,[165] Thurman agreed to freight supplies by wagon from his ranch in Mill Creek Canyon to the dam.

The Bear Valley Company, intending to go on with the work of the dam, purchased in June 1884, a four-horse load of provisions, to be taken there by S. Thurman, going up Mill Creek canyon and over the trail by burros. When crossing Mill creek, on June 13th, the wagon and load were all carried down the stream, and nothing saved from the wreck but one horse. Mr. Thurman, trying to loosen his horses from the wagon, was himself carried under it, and expected to lose his life, but was freed by the wagon overturning, and swam ashore. The water loosened the tugs in time to save one horse. This high water was caused by the sudden melting of the deep snow in the mountains.[166]

Brown and Thurman were an odd pair: Brown stout and bald and just five feet, two inches in height, and Thurman well over six feet tall. Frank Brown's constant promotion of "the largest man-made lake in the world"[167] and fundraising for ongoing projects meant that he hosted frequent pack trips for investors and the press to Bear Valley with his pal Thurman as guide. The mode of transportation sometimes elicited complaints, as the

Frank Brown and Sylvanus Thurman. *Courtesy Archives, A.K. Smiley Public Library.*

pack burros were famously flatulent, which Brown and Thurman apparently thought was hilarious. The fun would end, however, in 1889, as Thurman's closest relationships underwent dramatic changes. Amanda left Sylvanus against his will, and they went through a very contentious divorce. His good friend Frank Brown would also soon be lost to him. Following on the success of the Bear Valley Dam, Brown and the Bear Valley Irrigation Company were developing ambitious plans for another dam in Moreno Valley, making commitments for water to buyers of land. Regrettably, no investment and drought years from 1891 to 1893 put the company in receivership. Frank Brown left town under a cloud of censure.

Fortunately, Thurman prospered in his tourism business. Wilderness exploration by refugees from the crowded cities of the East drew thousands to the scenic heights of the San Bernardino Mountains for fishing, picnicking and excursions to the top of Mount San Gorgonio. Twice per week, a stagecoach took travelers to Thurman's Mill Creek ranch, and he guided them up the old miners' trail to Bluff Lake and Bear Valley on his burros.[168]

Sylvanus Thurman with burro train guests at Bluff Lake. *Courtesy Archives, A.K. Smiley Public Library.*

A female correspondent to the *Los Angeles Times* who was one of the guests on Thurman's pack train to Bluff Lake in 1891 described the experience as they arrived at his ranch.

> *Here there are several small buildings. Above the door of one, on a strip of canvas, is inscribed the word "Thurman's" (quite a well-known personage in these parts,) and here we have the first sight of a burro train.... The next morning, we rose at an early hour—we women folks in a nervous state, for we were to make our debut on the fiery and romantic burro. The burros had been promised at 7 o'clock in the morning, but as if to teach us a needed lesson in patience, they did not put in an appearance until 11 o'clock; when the whole train arrived, with half a dozen other Angelenos, all bound for Lewis's and Bear Valley. Our luggage, in canvas bags, (for that is the correct way to pack for the burro trains) and ourselves attired in costumes prepared for the trip, the ladies in short skirts, and belted blouses of brown and blue denim, with Knickerbockers of the same material, leather leggins and stout, comfortable shoes, with a soft felt hat, around which a veil was tied, completed a costume in which we were very comfortable. O dear! But*

what fears and inward quaking we felt, when with assistance we scrambled (no other word expresses it) into our saddles—that is we women—some on sidesaddles and others to ride man-fashion, which is considered the safest way....For a mile or so our trail led past several little farms nestling in the mountains. One place in particular known as "Forsee's" where the finest apples in Southern California are raised. In a short time, we crossed Mountain Home Creek. From this point on our trail led up the cañon along this beautiful stream for several miles....On, on we kept climbing until near Mountain Home summit, four and a half miles from Thurman's, we halted and dismounted and under a great pine tree partook of a light lunch, and rested our (by this time) weary limbs. Again mounting we soon reached the summit, which has an elevation of 5,700 feet....The timber on the summit is fine, one giant pine measuring thirty-three feet in circumference. We soon reached a point where we could overlook the basin of the Santa Ana River, which is lined for miles and miles with high, thickly-timbered mountains. Now our trials began, for the trail led down the mountain side and every turn it seemed to grow worse; it looked seemingly impossible but that we would go over the burros' heads. Finally, we found it more comfortable to trust ourselves to our feet....Each and every woman gave utterance to a sigh of relief, when we reached the Santa Ana River and comparatively level ground.

Among the eastern migrants coming to the Redlands area, Thurman found Mary Abbie Pillsbury, a teacher from Hampstead, New Hampshire, educated at Mount Holyoke Seminary[169] whose father came west to become an orange grower. Sylvanus and Abbie, as she was called, married in Redlands in 1893.

Thurman's entrepreneurial efforts paid off, and in November 1899, he secured a state land patent of 120 acres at Bluff Lake south of Bear Valley to develop a destination resort for his travelers.[170] J.M. Guinn described Thurman's resort and Mill Creek ranch in 1907.

Here he has erected log cabins and shake cabins which are used for cottages, Mr. Thurman himself conducting the dining room, running a dairy in connection with it and having his own beef to supply the table....He also owns four hundred and forty acres a mile from Crafton, and this property is devoted to the raising of hay, grain, and stock. He has an orchard on the place which supplies all his own fruits and also for market. There are eleven mountain springs on his ranch which supply ample water.

Left: Sylvanus Thurman and third wife Mary Abbie Pillsbury. *Courtesy Archives, A.K. Smiley Public Library.*

Below: Bluff Lake Resort. *Courtesy Archives, A.K. Smiley Public Library.*

Livestock had been part of Thurman's experience since he was a boy, and he remained a stockman throughout his life.[171] The U.S. government in 1909 tried an experiment using Angora goats to eat fire lanes through chaparral in the national forests and make space for planting marketable timber trees.[172] Capitalizing on this trend, and the value of the goats' coats, Thurman purchased two hundred Angoras that he put in the canyon and in the Crafton Hills in 1913. "There is a big demand for the wool from

Thurman, the old pioneer. *Courtesy Archives, A.K. Smiley Public Library.*

Angoras, it being used in the mohair on automobile tops, etc. It brings from 20 cents to $1 per pound, according to quality." Two years later, Thurman sold his Bluff Lake resort for $16,000 to a syndicate of men from the valley, and his Mill Creek goat business was thriving.[173]

The government has not been able to make a success of the goat fire brigade in the mountains, but Sylvanus Thurman is making a big success of his goat ranch in the mountains near here. Thurman now has a herd of 225 goats and he expects to add to this every year until he gets several thousand. Last year he sheared 200 pounds of wool from the smaller herd that he had and sold it to mills in Maine. The wool is of the mohair kind. Thurman has his goats in an enclosure of six miles of wire fence and has them trained so that they voluntarily come in every night from the mountains to be tucked into their little beds.[174]

The goats did actually prove useful on Yucaipa Ridge. Thurman marked off the width of a trail then staked the voracious creatures on a hillside and let them eat everything to the ground, moving them up the hillside each day until it formed a fire break.

After the sale of Bluff Lake, Thurman focused his time on living in Crafton with Abbie. The couple never had any children, but Abbie was active in the community, especially in charities. Giving up his resort in the high meadows

Damage to Thurman Flat, March 1938 flood. *Courtesy Archives, A.K. Smiley Public Library.*

may have signified that the mountain man's strength was waning, and he passed away on March 11, 1920, at the age of sixty-nine. Abbie followed him into death three years later at the age of eighty-three.[175]

Eighteen years after Thurman's death, the catastrophic flood of 1938 all but obliterated his homestead in the canyon, but his name lives on in a lovely, tree-shaded picnic area by Mill Creek in the San Bernardino National Forest.

7

KATE HARVEY

SIX-GUNS AND HUSBANDS

Bad choices make good stories.
—*Margaret Trudeau*

1888—Kate Harvey was the proprietress of Harvey's Mountain Home resort at present-day Loch Leven Camp and Retreat Center and was a pistol-packing legend who made headlines.

Kate Harvey told people that Powell Street in San Francisco was named for her father, Dr. John Goodson Powell.[176] It wasn't true, but it was a good story. John Powell from Tennessee was an itinerant dentist in the gold camps who dabbled in mining and occasional harness making.[177] He married twenty-year-old Hannah Sophia Keefer in Georgetown, El Dorado County, in 1862 when he was thirty-five years old, and they roamed from place to place with their daughter Mary Jessie, who was born in 1867.[178] A second daughter, Frances, died in 1872[179] in Sacramento. There wouldn't be another living child until they settled in San Bernardino, where Kate was born on February 17, 1877. Dr. and Mrs. Powell's last child and only son, Robert W. Powell, was born on January 23, 1880.[180] Sadly, Kate's father died on July 23, 1881, when Kate was four and Robert was only one year old.[181]

Kate Harvey's story in Mill Creek Canyon began with her mother's marriage to John W. Skinner, a disabled railroad man who moved to the

Right: Mary Jessie Powell, circa 1880.
Courtesy Debra Conn private collection.

Below: Young Kate Harvey with her brother Robert Powell, circa 1890. *Powell family private collection.*

mountains and squatted on land above Mountain Home Creek. Hannah and her children joined him there in December 1888, when Kate was eleven and Robert eight.[182] Their older sister, Jessie, had already married and was living in Redlands.[183] A journalist's colorful description in 1893 captured the personality of Kate's stepfather.

John Skinner, or "Uncle John," as he is familiarly known and spoken of, is a retired railroad contractor and used to be known from Oregon to San Diego. As he frequently tells it, he was "broke" when he came to San Bernardino County, but when pressed, acknowledges that he actually had a dollar and a quarter when he settled on the pleasant little spot four years ago [1888] where he now has his home. After he had been there some time, Will Hope of San Bernardino gave him a three-legged horse and he rigged up a couple of tugs into a breast-strap of hay and gunnysacks, and prepared to cut roots. For want of a plow he cut an alder sapling in such a way as to use two of the branches, when trimmed down, for handles. To this he bolted a sharpened piece of steel that resembles a Chinese meat axe, and cleared the beautiful spot which is now occupied by his mountain home.[184]

Skinner was a character but also an educated man who had been a schoolteacher in his home state of Ohio before he went railroading west. Understanding that his rustic home inclined people to think he was a hick, he'd play along. "In fact, it's amusement for him to assume the character of a backwoods Missourian with a drollery and artfulness that immediately captivates the congressman, banker or tourist that happens to stop with him. Said he, 'why they won't have it any other way. They come here expecting me to say "keow" for cow, and "guessan' cakilate a right smart" and "sich stuff" and nothing else'll go, so I say it, and I reckon they think I don't know any better.'"

The Skinners' home was a popular rest stop for travelers who followed the trail up the canyon to the Santa Ana River and Seven Oaks or farther on to Bear Valley. Soon, it became a popular tent camping resort in Mill Creek Canyon at the terminus of the stage route.[185] Skinner's featured Hannah's home cooking, and Kate and Bob helped out with guests and farming their orchards and fields. In September 1890, John Skinner transferred his possessory claim, or squatter's rights, to Hannah, giving her what amounted to a deed to his land.[186] Notably, the circumstances and documentation of their marriage are a bit murky, but John Skinner frequently referred to Hannah as Mrs. J.W. Skinner.[187]

In 1894, John applied to have a post office, which would have given Mill Creek Canyon its first official town name of Skinner, California, but he withdrew the application before it could be granted by the government.[188] One of the reasons he may have withdrawn that application is that he suddenly came under intense scrutiny. The landowners in the valley below claimed they owned the rights to all of the water in Mill Creek and its tributary streams, which were diverted into the Mill Creek *zanja* and used by them for irrigation.[189] Rancher Benjamin Cave filed suit against the Skinners and the other ranchers in Mill Creek Canyon in 1897, alleging that they were stealing water by diverting it for the irrigation of their own crops and domestic use. As a squatter, John Skinner knew that his rights were tenuous, and every time someone came to inspect their water usage, he affirmed that he didn't have a right to divert water.[190] However, the inspectors noted that Skinner's crops were always green and healthy, and John Skinner and Bob Powell made something of a game of trying to outsmart the inspectors. Courtship games were also in progress at Skinner's, and in March of that year, at the age of seventeen, Kate married thirty-one-year-old Lue Harvey, who helped out on the ranch as a laborer.

Although the journalist who stopped at Skinner's noted that "Uncle John is nearing sixty years of age, but exhibits a rugged constitution and activity that might easily be taken for a man of forty, notwithstanding he is disabled by a badly crippled arm," one wonders if he transferred his property under duress from Hannah or because his health was failing. The water lawsuit dragged on for three years, during which time John Skinner died.[191] Kate's mother was still fighting the case when she, too, died on January 25, 1901.[192] As executrix of her mother's estate, Kate continued the legal battle in her mother's place. It was years before it would be resolved, but that was just the start of Kate's troubles.

On the day of Hannah's death, Lue Harvey appeared to offer compassion when he said to a grieving Bob Powell, "We'll let all this business of property affairs go until later, for it wouldn't be right to try to settle up such matters so soon after your mother's death."[193] Unbeknownst to Powell, Lue had already gone through Hannah's trunk and found her will, which left all of her property to her son Bob. Powell was offered $7,000 for what he believed was his half interest in Skinner's ranch by an investor, but instead, he accepted $400 from his brother-in-law, thinking that if the property was in Harvey's name, Kate would ultimately benefit. Interestingly, Powell had married a girl named Grace Greenlee shortly after his mother's death, and the following year they had a son, Norman, which makes it somewhat surprising that he would forego his own family's security in favor of his sister's.[194]

A few months later, a local man disclosed Harvey's dirty trick to Powell. The feud was on between Kate's brother and her husband. Enmity smoldered dangerously while John Harvey, Lue's brother, moved in. And Powell was also going through a heated divorce and custody battle with Grace. Bob watched helplessly while Lue and his shiftless brother John abused Kate for eight years. Powell continually insisted that John Harvey had to leave, and Lue taunted him, saying, "If you can make him, go to it."

On December 21, 1910, Kate phoned her brother, her voice desperate, and Powell rushed to her home. The Harvey brothers were on the porch, and Powell fired shots, killing John Harvey, then he took Kate to a neighboring ranch, where he calmly waited for the sheriff to come and arrest him. "I shot and killed John Harvey intentionally and deliberately. He was the man I wanted to get, and I got him, and that's all there is to it, and I will say so if I get my neck cracked. All I want is a jury trial, and I don't care what they do with me," Powell said to reporters the next day from his jail cell. The front pages of newspapers throughout Southern California shouted that Kate, the pretty young wife, was kept in abject slavery by her husband and his brother.[195] "They forced her to do all the drudgery on the Mill creek canyon ranch, and when she was overcome by exhaustion and fatigue beatings and abuse forced her to the hard tasks which they demanded she perform."

Powell's trial began on April 4, 1911, and new elements came to light, namely that "liquor was as common to the Harvey boys as water," and that before the shooting incident, Kate had been made so despondent by her plight that she had attempted suicide.[196] However, she was also shown to be quite a cool head in a pinch. "Lue Harvey, who had appeared on the porch, ran back into the house, and entering Mrs. Harvey's room sought a revolver, but she, leaving her bed on hearing him say that Powell was shooting at them, secured the weapon and dropped it into an overcoat pocket" then fled. The trial aroused intense interest, with days of "shocking" testimony about Kate's life with her husband and brother-in-law. Ultimately, Kate and Bob won the sympathies of the jury, which acquitted Powell of the murder of John Harvey in a record ten minutes.[197]

The experience gave Kate the will to file for a divorce from Lue Harvey, which was granted on June 19, 1911.[198] From that point on, she began to take on the status of a tragic but brave heroine in the press. One report tells of her rescue in an avalanche in 1912.[199] Another story had her facing down an enormous mountain lion.[200] One begins to suspect that, whether or not the stories were true, Kate Harvey just made good copy. Regardless, at the age of thirty-four, Kate began to thrive, as did the resort she'd inherited.

For a girl who'd always had a short supply of luck, Kate received an enormous windfall with the advent of the automobile. People in Southern California were crazy for cars, and they were beginning to demand better

Kate Harvey's Mountain Home Resort. *Courtesy Archives, A.K. Smiley Public Library.*

roads for scenic trips.[201] The San Bernardino County supervisors approved funding for the first road into the mountains, and the route began in Mill Creek Canyon, traveling right through Kate's property.[202] As soon as the one-lane road opened in 1914, the traffic went up once per day and came down once per day, which meant that travelers had to camp while they waited in line for their turn to use the control road to Bear Valley. Kate's resort and dining hall business was brisk. She was also given the job of policing the toll gate, and she did so with loaded pistols strapped around her ample hips. Locals said that you couldn't find a bigger heart or more generous soul than "Cactus" Kate, as they called her, but they would always add, "you wouldn't want to cross her though," and she was well known for having a very blue vocabulary when she was riled.[203]

Unfortunately, Kate's luck proved fickle. On February 3, 1916, newspapers broke devastating news. "The first authentic word was received in Mentone today concerning the devastation wrought by the recent storm at Mountain Home. Judging by the reports brought in by Ranger Jack Allen, the flood must have been a wonder even to the seasoned residents of Mill Creek canyon. Mr. Allen gave the statement that Mrs. Kate Harvey had sustained the loss of practically everything she possessed at her mountain home. Her

Sign stating the rules of the control road, circa 1920. *Courtesy Mark Durban private collection.*

Travelers waiting at Kate Harvey's control, circa 1920. *Courtesy Mark Durban private collection.*

entire boarding establishment, including the kitchen, dining room and all her tent houses, in fact all she had was swept away in the flood."[204]

Although her losses had been severe, Kate rebuilt, and she didn't spook easily. Her next escapade demonstrates that she must also have been a romantic at heart. On July 11, 1918, at the age of forty-one, Kate became a war bride, marrying William D. Howard, who was reporting for duty in World War I a week after their wedding.[205] "Mrs. Howard will remain on the ranch with her brother, who has made his home with her for several years. The marriage of Mrs. Harvey will come as a great surprise to her many friends and acquaintances, who have only thought of her as the genial lady who has presided all these years over the romantic spot known first as Skinner's and later as Harvey's."

William Howard's service was short, and he was home by their first anniversary in July 1919, when Kate's life took a bizarre U-turn.[206] During dinner on July 14, an argument broke out between Bob Powell and Kate's husband over some cows that Kate had mortgaged. Howard accused Powell of selling them, and Bob pulled his revolver. Kate, fearing what he might do, jumped up to stand in front of her husband, but Powell fired. The bullet entered Kate's left arm, shattering the bone, then hit Howard underneath his right eye. As he had before, Powell waited patiently to be arrested while Kate and William were taken to the hospital. Kate and her brother returned to their refrain of terrible abuse, but Howard averred. "I never did such a thing," he said. "The people of the canyon, and the people of Redlands, know better than that. She loves me and I love her and when I can talk with her, she will change her attitude. She doesn't know all. Her brother has threatened to kill her. That house, from which I ordered Powell, is my house. I built it, and I can prove that he did sell four of his sister's cows that were mortgaged."[207] Again, Kate chose to stand by her brother, which strangely may have been the wise choice. During the trial, she testified that her husband had told her he killed a man in Alaska, and it was revealed that William D. Howard was an alias. His true name was Richard N. Reeves.[208]

After the trial, Powell left for the Whitewater wilderness beyond the Mill Creek Jumpoff at the end of the canyon to take up trapping and live alone.[209] Kate struggled along with her resort for the next several years then sold the 160 acres to a real estate syndicate in 1926.[210] The new owners planned to subdivide 40 acres for homes and develop the remaining 120 acres for sports and recreation as the posh Dolly Varden Angling Club, which is now Loch Leven Camp and Retreat Center.[211]

By 1937, Kate had been missing from the headlines for more than a decade when she reemerged in the spotlight in yet another harrowing tale. On January 11, eight people were reported to have been trapped in the remote Onyx Mine in Pipes Canyon since Christmas.[212] One member of the party had snowshoed out on boards found in the mine and flagged down a driver on the highway. He said that their food supplies had run out four days before. The only person identified among the marooned party north of Whitewater was Kate Harvey, who was working as the cook at the mine. Kate had been living at Onyx since at least 1930 with her old friend from Mill Creek Canyon, Tom Akers, one of the founders of Forest Home.[213] Various reports spoke of Kate's declining health, and there was one more headline for the old girl to make. While still living in a remote cabin in Pipes Canyon, Kate had a stroke and lay helpless there for some time. A man who was camping nearby found her and took her to the hospital in San Bernardino.

Kate's life, which had inspired so many sensational headlines, ended on July 11, 1944.[214] She was sixty-seven years old. The smallest of mentions marked her passing in the newspaper, but her legend grew over the years with the telling and retelling of her larger-than-life story.

Her brother, Robert Powell, died on May 22, 1960, in Nevada City, California, at the age of eighty.[215]

RICHARD JACKSON AND THOMAS AKERS

FOREST HOME RESORT AND AKERS' CAMP

Borrow trouble for yourself, if that's your nature,
but don't lend it to your neighbors.
—Rudyard Kipling

1896—Richard Jackson established the original Forest Home Resort on his family ranch in Mill Creek Canyon, but his brother-in-law Thomas Akers made it famous.

Larkin Braxton Akers and Catherine Beasley Holladay, daughter of famed plantation owner and California pioneer John Holladay, came to California by wagon train in 1856 from Hamilton, Marion County, Alabama. The couple had fourteen children, seven girls and seven boys. At first, they settled in San Bernardino then went to Los Angeles and by the mid-1870s were in Lone Pine in Inyo County, farming. They returned to the Inland Empire, where they and their children permanently settled.

It's uncertain exactly how the Jackson and Akers families met, but between 1892 and 1898, Thomas Akers, Larkin and Catherine's seventh child, was a rancher in Crafton.[216] Richard Jackson had lived in Mill Creek Canyon since he was seven years old; for him, it truly was his forest home.[217] After his mother, Elizabeth Jackson Petty's, death in 1893, Richard became a landed young gent as one of her heirs, running the Jackson ranch with his brother

Larkin and Catherine Akers with their seven sons, circa 1875, Lone Pine. *Seated from left to right*: Franklin, Larkin, Catherine, John and Richard. *Standing from left to right*: Oregon, William, Thomas and David. *Courtesy San Bernardino Public Library, with thanks to Mrs. Donna Weppler.*

Lee.[218] In August 1895, Richard married Minnie Belle Akers, Tom Akers's youngest sister, which joined the two families as in-laws.[219]

Tom Akers probably had more southern charm and good looks than he should have been allowed. Certainly, he had more temper and intense passions than he knew what to do with, and those traits seem to have been shared by other family members. Some of the Akers siblings did their level best to consume gallons of printers' ink in the newspapers with their scandals, misdeeds and shocking lifestyles. Tom's brother David, who was two years younger, went to jail for beating his wife, but many defended him, as it seems his wife had been too intimate with their nineteen-year-old nephew—an affair that carried on while David Akers was in jail, subsequently resulting in the nephew's arrest.[220] The youngest brother, Franklin, who was a teamster, attempted suicide with whisky and laudanum in 1893; four years later, he, too, got into trouble for domestic abuse.[221]

Frank and his family lived in such squalor that "the officers were shocked at the total absence of anything that suggested comfort or decency." Older brother William went to Folsom prison for five years, because, as the *Los Angeles Herald* put it, he was "in the horse-borrowing business."[222] Most notorious, however, were Martha and Mary Akers, who worked out of the French-American Hotel in San Bernardino and were known to "stand in the open windows and call to men passing along the street to come up." They reportedly "acquired considerable fame as street walkers."[223] The *Weekly Courier* did, however, go to the trouble of saying that not all Akers women were a blight on the town, just those two.[224]

Richard Jackson, perhaps influenced by the successful tourism of his friend Sylvanus Thurman, opened up a wilderness resort on the forested upper part of his ranch around 1896. Twice per week, on Tuesdays and Fridays, he drove down the rocky reaches of Mill Creek Canyon in a horse-drawn stage, crossing the creek again and again to pick up guests at the Barker House in Redlands and then make the hours-long return journey.[225]

On July 5, 1897, at the age of forty-four, Tom Akers married a very young Florinda Belle Crain in San Jacinto, where he had a home.[226] That

Forest Home stage, circa 1890s. *Courtesy Archives, A.K. Smiley Public Library.*

Summit of Grayback, Theodore Parker Lukens, 1898. *Courtesy California State Library.*

same summer, Richard Jackson began to advertise his Forest Home resort, and an August article in the *San Bernardino Weekly Sun* offers a glimpse of his business, describing "the campers who throng Mill Creek Cañon."[227] The article profiles a lively party of ten ladies and gents making the ascent of Old Grayback on burros. Tom Akers was among them, but curiously, his bride was not. "The party left Forest Home, Richard Jackson's resort, at 9 o'clock Friday morning, and barring the killing of a rattlesnake, with but two rattles and a button, and the bestowing of names on the burros, the next four hours were uneventful. Arriving at Lily valley [Vivian Creek meadows], the party halted for lunch. The name was selected by the party because the valley was a fragrant bed of yellow lilies. After lunch they mounted, and for three hours longer the burros toiled toward Greyback."

The campers stayed on the summit overnight but, finding it too cold, scurried back down the mountain as dawn broke. Akers must have been impressed by the journey, because he filed a homestead claim for 160 acres east up the canyon from Jackson's property on the same day Richard and George Jackson filed for theirs, July 27, 1897.[228] By that fall, Tom was already making improvements at "Akers Camp."[229]

Akers was enterprising, simultaneously running a boardinghouse with Florinda in Redlands, his camp in Mill Creek Canyon and a wood business.[230] He appeared to be flush with cash, as he was making mortgages and purchased commercial property at the southwest corner of Stuart Avenue between Sixth and Seventh Streets in Redlands on which he intended to build a hotel.[231] Tom had experience with hospitality and, perhaps, an aptitude for it. Richard Jackson, on the other hand, didn't care much for being a host and preferred ranching on his own homestead. He faded away from running Forest Home and, instead, went to work for the Redlands Electric Light and Power Company with his older brother, George.

By 1898, the resort Jackson established was widely known as Akers' Forest Home. Tom was well aware that travel to the summit of Old Grayback was a big draw for his resort business, and he hired Martin and Albert Vivian to cut a trail through the thick brush up the mountainside to Mount San Gorgonio that year. The Vivian brothers were first cousins of the Jacksons, their mother being Elizabeth Jackson's youngest sister, Martha Archer Vivian.[232] The family connection no doubt got them the job. The Vivians had been knocking around, trying some mining without much success and may have appreciated the steady work, despite how grueling it must have been.* Akers also hired Nathan and Margaret Jellison to help him run Forest Home. Nathan managed the wood business and expanded the amenities with his building and carpentry skills while Margaret served as hostess, housekeeper and general manager with the help of their daughter.[233] Frequent ads extolled the virtues of Forest Home under their management. "FOREST HOME HOTEL—This beautiful Summer Resort is situated in Mill Creek Canyon, 17 miles from Redlands. Elevation 5,190; plenty of fresh milk, butter and eggs; price per day $1. Mrs. Maggie Jellison Proprietress."

Mrs. Jellison's fresh milk came from cattle Akers kept down on the Jacksons' big pastureland along Mill Creek below his resort. Large canisters were loaded onto donkeys in the morning and taken to the meadow to be filled during milking.[234] Not having to bring one's own cow for a holiday in the mountains (some people did!) was a big enticement, and whether it was the fresh dairy, abundant trout fishing or the idyllic, lush forested scenery, Forest Home resort was becoming well known throughout the Southland.

Akers stayed with the Jellisons when he was in the canyon, but soon, close quarters got on all of their nerves. On August 30, 1900, a quarrel started

---

* The Vivian brothers earned a place in history with their hard work, giving their name to Vivian Creek, Vivian Falls and the Vivian Creek Trail.

Left: Forest Home "Milk Wagon." *Courtesy Tom Atchley private collection.*

Below: Fine accommodations at Forest Home Resort, circa 1910. *Courtesy Archives, A.K. Smiley Public Library.*

in the orchard between Tom and Maggie Jellison, with anger continuing to seethe when they returned to the house. According to Mrs. Jellison:

> *I asked him to let me move the chair to pass and he kept using vile language. When he wouldn't let me move the chair, I said, "Mr. Akers, you have been aching for a row or for a fuss all the forenoon, you dirty scrub." My daughter was standing at his left side trying to get him to be quiet, and stop using such vile language as there were strangers boarding there and he called*

me a vile name and struck me in the face. I told him I wouldn't take that
from any man and hit him. Then he hit me a second blow, bruising my face
and knocking out a tooth.[235]

Tom's story differed, alleging that Mrs. Jellison started the whole thing when "she picked up a crib board and hit me plump across the nose with it."[236] His perspective was that it was all a setup for money and that he only struck out in self-defense when the three Jellisons ganged up on him. Admittedly, the *Evening Transcript*, which printed both of these stories, did have a tendency toward the sensational, but the fact remained that it was a pitched battle in the courts with suits and countersuits and enormous legal bills mounting.[237] As a result, Akers soon needed to raise money. He began to sell property, and it became clear that even Forest Home would have to go. He made an agreement with Eugene S. Libby, a real estate investor, to buy his Mill Creek Canyon property with a down payment of $150. Libby had ninety days to pay the balance, but he defaulted.[238] Instead, Akers sold his mountain resort to Cyrus G. Baldwin.[239]

In the end, the court ordered Akers to pay $80.02 to Nathan Jellison. However, his finances were ruined by legal costs, and by that time, the Jellisons were the least of Tom Akers's personal and legal troubles.

On July 6, 1902, Tom returned to his home in San Jacinto to find his wife, Florinda, in a flagrantly compromising situation with another man.[240] Florinda fled with her lover to Pomona, leaving Earl, the Akerses' two-year-old son, behind. Tom arranged for his sister Nora to take Earl temporarily, but the following month, Florinda snatched the boy on the street from Nora's husband, J.J. Arbios, and there was a struggle. Everyone went to court, little Earl's wide eyes and bewilderment haunting them, while Tom impugned his wife's character, calling her immoral and unfit to raise a child. By the end of the month, the Akerses, seeing their little boy in such distress in court, agreed to reconcile. The reconciliation didn't last; they divorced in 1904, and Florinda was given custody. "One day she disappeared with a young fellow, and the stories that reached [Akers] took him to Trinity county, where he kidnapped the child. Akers had a long and hazardous tramp across mountains of that wild country, carrying the little one on his shoulders for miles before reaching a railroad point, and he hastened [to San Bernardino], where the child was placed with relatives."[241]

Earl was surreptitiously passed among members of the Akers family just ahead of police and sheriffs' posses who were looking for him, and one of Tom's relatives managed to sneak the four-year-old through the brush from

Lytle Creek to the train in Bloomington, where Tom was waiting. He took Earl to Santa Monica and then to Tuolumne County. Ultimately, after weeks of sensational type in the newspapers and the most shocking kidnapping case in the county's history, the courts awarded custody of Earl to Tom's sister Melisia Mettler.[242] Florinda remarried a year later.

Tom was never really the same after that. He wandered through years and jobs that kept him in the mountain forests for the remainder of his life.[243] In 1930, at the age of seventy-seven, Akers was living in remote Pipes Canyon at the camp for the Onyx Mine, working as a watchman. The only thing he had left was a long friendship with Mill Creek Canyon's most legendary woman, Kate Harvey, with whom he was living. Seven years later, Thomas Akers died at the age of eighty-four.

RACHEL TYLER

WOMEN AND WATER FIND THEIR WAY

Without water our land would be worthless.
—*Mary C. Vail,* Both Sides Told, or California As It Is, *1888*

1892—Rachel M. Tyler and her son George W. Tyler purchased the Peter Forsee homestead and turned it into Tyler's Mountain Resort.

Rachel Tyler's journey from tender girl to tough pioneer woman is a tale of fortitude and cleverness. The roots of her story reach back to before the San Bernardino Colony and toward the cusp of the Jazz Age in a shiny new twentieth century that would transform Mill Creek Canyon.

Born Rachel Melinda Moore on August 26, 1842, in Nauvoo, Illinois,[244] her parents, John Harvey Moore and Clarissa Drollinger, fled Nauvoo during the Mormon exodus from that city in 1846 when Rachel was three years old and her younger sister, Rebecca, was one. On the banks of the Missouri River in Pottawattamie County, Iowa, they waited for more than five years to be called to Utah. When Rachel was nine, the family left with the Thomas C.D. Howell wagon train for Salt Lake. Her sister Rebecca Estella Moore recalls the journey.

There was heavy emigration that summer, both of Saints and gold-seekers. The cholera was bad, but we didn't get it in our company. There were fresh graves all along the way for miles. In one place wolves had dug up a body; it was lying by the side of a grave. The men got their shovels and buried it again....When we came to the foot of the big mountain, we camped there one Sunday. The men killed a buffalo and took oxen to drag it into camp so we could all see it. I remember that the meat tasted very good. There was a great pile of wagon irons there, and we thought there had been a company of emigrants killed by the Indians, who had also burned the wagons.[245]

The Moores settled in Payson, Utah, where, on Valentine's Day 1857, at the age of fourteen and a half, Rachel became a bride to Charles Brent Hancock, thirty-four.[246] She was one of two brides that day in a plural marriage and was his fourth simultaneous wife.[247] By 1860, she had two children, daughter Melinda Jane and son George Wesley, but a different future was waiting for her in the person of Uriah Urban Tyler, who'd been living in the San Bernardino Valley since 1848.[248] It must have taken some courage to divorce Charles Hancock, but she did so and married Uriah Tyler on May 17, 1865, in Salt Lake City. Rachel's daughter, Melinda,

Rachel Tyler with her parents and siblings, circa 1880s. *Seated from left to right:* Rebecca Tanner, Rachel Tyler, John Moore and Clarissa Moore. *Standing from left to right:* Clarissa Jane Moore, Annie Huish, John Moore Jr. and George B. Moore. *Courtesy Mr. and Mrs. Ben A. Reeves private collection.*

Uriah Urban Tyler. *J.M. Guinn, A History of California, 1907.*

shared her recollections about that period in her life. "When between seven and eight years of age, I went with my mother and foster [step] father from Payson over the Southern Desert, to San Bernardino, California. This was a great trial to leave my dear old great-grandmother, grandparents, and also my dear father. However, my foster father, U.U. Tyler was very good and kind to me. (A father in every deed) for ten years."[249]

Indeed, Rachel's son George always used the name Tyler and was never known as Hancock after arriving in California.[250] At San Bernardino, Uriah Tyler was well established. In 1852, he assisted surveyor Henry Washington in establishing the San Bernardino Meridian survey point on top of the 10,649-foot peak of Mount San Bernardino. He was also the first to drive the mail between Los Angeles and San Bernardino and sometimes took passengers in the early days.[251] Tyler had the only butcher shop in the area; when the Mormons left, he took up positions of importance, serving as the first justice of the peace and an elected deputy sheriff. In 1859, he became the San Bernardino County assessor.[252] Uriah and his brother Charles Y. Tyler, whom he'd gone adventuring to California with, established farms in the north end of San Bernardino along E Street. Charles had some success as a gold miner in Holcomb Valley.[253]

One has the sense that Uriah and Rachel were a love match, and they quickly increased their family with a daughter, Elizabeth Ann, known as Lizzy, born while they were still in Payson, Utah,[254] and four sons, Emery Brainard, Urban Amasa, John Hugh and Guy Edward, all born in San Bernardino. They also increased their real estate portfolio with acquisitions including a large ranch compound at Second Street and Arrowhead Avenue in San Bernardino[255] on the former site of the Lugo hacienda and holdings beyond the valley with considerable farming and livestock. It was a robust start to their marriage, but heartache was coming. In 1876, their one-year-old son, Guy, died, and six years later, on July 2, 1882, at the age of fifty-six, Uriah would also leave life and Rachel behind.[256]

By the time of Uriah's death, twenty-two-year-old George Tyler had taken up his stepfather's business, working as a butcher in Colton and later

Seated from left to right: Clarissa Moore, Rachel Mary Cook and Rachel Tyler. *Standing from left to right*: Clarissa Rawson and Melinda Hancock Rawson, Rachel's eldest daughter. *Courtesy Tracie DeRoche private collection.*

serving as a constable in that city, becoming politically connected there.[257] In 1887, when Colton incorporated and Virgil Earp of Tombstone fame was appointed marshal, George was on the first board of trustees.[258] He would have been quite familiar with Colton's famous marble and limestone quarry at Slover Mountain and perhaps saw the financial potential of quarrying stone. In 1889, Major J.F. Sterling, a wealthy businessman from

E Street, San Bernardino, looking north, circa 1900. *Courtesy Ana Bégué de Packman Papers, Charles E Young Research Library, UCLA.*

Philadelphia, purchased all of the land on both sides of Mill Creek just below Sylvanus Thurman's property to the mouth of the canyon from W.C. Clark.[259] The section was much narrower then and lined by sandstone cliffs. "Shortly after his arrival in California Mr. Sterling took up his residence in Colton. Here, with a number of Los Angeles and San Bernardino men, he began to operate in building stone."[260] One of those men was George Tyler, who became the vice-president and general manager and invested $10,000[261] in the Mentone Sandstone Company. George was not an easy partner, and he could be legally hair-triggered when he thought he was wronged, but the enterprise started with enthusiastic boosterism by the press and local business.

> *The company working and developing the stone quary [sic] on Mill Creek, above Mentone, are getting out considerable rock, most of which is being sent to Los Angeles and being used for building purposes in that city. The company has purchased a large tract of land and the water rights for power. They intend to erect a mill for the dressing of the stone and will utilize the power to run their machinery. The quantity of stone is said to be almost unlimited and of a superior quality and becoming very popular in Los Angeles and other places where it has been used.[262]*

Mill Creek Canyon sandstone cliffs, circa 1900. *Courtesy Archives, A.K. Smiley Public Library.*

The Mentone Sandstone Company, which was significantly changing the landscape in Mill Creek Canyon, landed a contract for the new San Bernardino Hall of Records and County Courthouse as well as buildings and homes in Redlands and throughout the Los Angeles area.[263] The quarry seems to be one of the factors that shifted the focus of Rachel and George Tyler's lives toward Mill Creek Canyon. Another may have been the events of Sunday afternoon, April 13, 1890.

> *About 3 o'clock fire broke out in the dwelling house of Mrs. Tyler, on Second street, between C and D streets, and in a few minutes the building was a mass of smoking embers. The origin of the fire is a mystery, as none of the stoves has been in use for several hours. The belief is that spontaneous combustion in a clothes room was the cause. The fire had such a start when discovered that nothing could be done to save the building or contents, except a piano and some furniture in the parlor.*[264]

Rachel would have to start over again. George soon found himself in a difficult position, too. In the early hours of January 15, 1892, Major Sterling, the president of the Mentone Sandstone Company, shot himself in the chest with his pistol while in his room at the Transcontinental Hotel in Colton, avowing his intent to commit suicide. He succeeded after lingering for more

Old San Bernardino County Courthouse. *Courtesy San Bernardino Public Library.*

than a day. Sterling left a letter saying that he was tired of life and that his business affairs were in a terrible mess. This left the company, George Tyler and David Kilpatrick, the other active business partner, in a bind. Aggressive advertising throughout that year with George's name emblazoned on the ads as the general manager may suggest that the Mill Creek sandstone quarry was consuming more of his time than he'd anticipated.

George Tyler purchased the Peter Forsee ranch and orchards in Mill Creek Canyon from Martha McHaney Forsee and deeded the property to his mother in June 1892.[265] They promptly took up residence together at the ranch with Rachel's youngest son, John.[266] Mrs. Tyler set about making the ranch into "Tyler's Mountain Resort," advertising "good fishing and hunting," with a "stage twice a week to and from Redlands during the summer months."[267]

History doesn't tell us whether the few neighbors in the area greeted them with pies and a howdy-do, but it is certain that things would soon become very contentious in the canyon over the issue of water. To say that Rachel Tyler and her son George were litigious is an understatement of magnitudes. Fortunately, Rachel's son Emery studied law at the University of Michigan and became a lawyer.[268] They certainly needed one in the family. George sued people at a steady clip for everything from the sale of a white mule that ended in gunplay to unpaid debts.[269] However, the real troubles began on September 18, 1894, when Benjamin W. Cave and fifty-one other plaintiffs filed suit against the Tylers and fourteen other defendants, alleging that they were illegally taking water from Mill Creek for their personal use.[270] Cave and the others were landowners along the Mill Creek *zanja*, an irrigation canal that had been used almost continuously since the days of the Spanish missions by agriculturists and households in the valley below Mill Creek Canyon. The Tylers maintained that the water rights had come with the land when purchased from the Southern Pacific Railroad. Rachel Tyler sued neighbor Elizabeth Petty[271] over water rights, engendering a battle of the pioneer women, and the Barton Land and Water Company, et al., took Rachel to court in 1899. These suits were litigated for years, and just as they were coming to resolution (some in the Supreme Court of California) with findings generally not in the Tylers' favor, George and his mother filed suit against the Edison Power Company in 1902.[272]

The world outside Mill Creek Canyon was changing dramatically as it raced toward a new century, and technology on Mill Creek would leave as great an imprint on the world as the quarry had on the canyon. Direct current, or DC, power had been introduced in the Southland in the 1880s but would only transmit three to five miles from the generating plant.[273] Spoilage was a problem for Redlands' citrus growers, and they needed ice to refrigerate their crops, which the Union Ice Company was prepared to supply. Unfortunately, DC power couldn't provide enough electricity to satisfy the demand. Henry Harbison Sinclair and a group of businessmen incorporated the Redlands Light and Power Company in 1891 to solve this

The Tylers' home and barns, 1918. *Courtesy Southern California Edison Collection.*

Forsee's orchards on the Tyler Ranch, 1918. *Courtesy Southern California Edison Collection.*

problem and hired a young, tubercular electrical engineer named Almarian W. Decker.[274] Decker was aware of the multiphase power work of Nicola Tesla and others and suggested alternating current, or AC, power as a solution. On September 7, 1893, the world's first three-phase power was generated on Mill Creek, and AC power continues to power much of the world. Although this was an extraordinary development for America, it was the beginning of the end for the Tylers' mountain resort. Mill Creek powered the electrical system, which meant that the power company took water out of its flow into their holding tanks at their generating stations and the Tylers were competing for water for their orchards and livestock. The Tylers' suit against the electric company to regain their water failed.

In 1903, the Tylers sold their Mill Creek ranch and bought a home on Second Street in San Bernardino.[275] Rachel took up the cause of crusading against the red-light district and houses of ill repute in San Bernardino.[276] George, who was no longer involved with the Mentone Sandstone Company, had amassed vast ranchlands north of Rialto and in the Victor Valley, with enormous herds of horses and cattle as well as interests in mining and oil exploration.[277]

In 1908, a failing Rachel asked her daughter, Lizzie, to come from her home in Portland, Oregon, to care for her. Lizzie was married and had a young daughter, but she came to be by her mother's side as Rachel's health declined.[278] On May 28, 1913, Rachel Tyler died quietly at her home in San Bernardino;[279] she was seventy years old.

George, who always seemed to be surrounded by suspicious fires and peculiar events, including finding large jars of gold coins and a giant skeleton beneath his land on Second Street in San Bernardino, never married.[280] He lived a long life, finally succumbing at the age of eighty-one in 1943. Emery, who was something of a social darling in Redlands in his youth, inherited his father, Uriah's, adventurous spirit and went prospecting in Nome, Alaska, before settling into life as a prominent lawyer in San Bernardino. He, too, remained unmarried.[281] Both Urban and John married, had families and spent their lives in the area as farmers and ranchers.[282]

Rachel Tyler's life was exemplary of the pioneer woman's experience of hardships and obstacles, but like the waters of Mill Creek that she fought so hard for, she found her way. In the end, as noted in her obituary, "one of the oldest residents of the city passed on to join the other pioneers who have crossed the last divide."

JOHN W. DOBBS AND CYRUS G. BALDWIN

TRAILBLAZERS AND ELECTRIC DREAMS

Vision without execution is hallucination.
—*Thomas Edison*

1896—John W. Dobbs left his mark on Mill Creek Canyon with his name on Dobbs Peak, Dobbs Cabin, Dobbs Camp and Dobbs flume, through which his legacy lives on.

The upper reaches of Mill Creek Canyon were a relatively pristine wilderness in the final decade of the nineteenth century. No real road led beyond Akers' Forest Home, and the creek bed down the middle of the canyon was a mass of trees and shrubs that was so dense it was very easy to get lost in.[283] Campers found their way to sylvan spots of their choosing by contending with the rocky trails and bushwhacking to reach their destinations. As the twentieth century approached, all of that would change drastically, and John Dobbs was an agent of that change.

Born in Benton, Saline County, Arkansas, on June 22, 1856, Dobbs rambled to Texas as a young man.[284] There, he became a water-well digger and married his bride, Josephine Bolen, in 1883 in Waco.[285] John moved his family to California in 1896, trying Long Beach first then Redlands. He arrived right around the time the first official survey into Mill Creek Canyon was accepted and land was opening up, either for sale through the Southern

Campers along Mill Creek, circa 1900. *Courtesy Archives, A.K. Smiley Public Library.*

Pacific Railroad or by homestead patent through the U.S. government.[286] Although prospectors filed many claims, hoping to exploit mineral rights,[287] the gold rush never happened in Mill Creek Canyon, but a rush of a different sort was on with hydroelectric power. Electricity was making the fortunes of men like Henry Harbison Sinclair with his Redlands Electric Light and Power Company and Cyrus G. Baldwin, Sinclair's erstwhile partner, who founded the San Antonio Light and Power Company.[288]

Baldwin, an unlikely electrical pioneer, was a Congregationalist minister and the former first president of Pomona College. He had developed the first hydroelectric power generation in Southern California at his San Antonio Canyon power plant near Claremont, California, transmitting direct current power over a long distance—twenty-nine miles—for the first time on November 28, 1892.[289] Sinclair's Mill Creek power plant generated the first three-phase AC power almost a year later.[290] Assuredly, electricity was the talk of the town when John Dobbs arrived in Redlands, and he quickly got into the game.[291]

On November 7, 1897, Dobbs filed a claim on 150 inches and 200 inches of water for surface and underflow rights, respectively, to tributaries on the north side of Mill Creek Canyon. It was noted: "Dobbs proposes to conduct this water in an open ditch and flume one foot wide and two feet deep, and a 10-inch steel pipe to a point on the north side of Mill creek, opposite T.R. Akers' house, there to be used to generate electricity to be used at Lakeview, Perris, Menifee and Elsinore for pumping water, for light, heat, etc. for the inhabitants of said places."[292]

It was a bold move, but as a newcomer, Dobbs may not have been aware of the long and contentious legal battles over water in the canyon that had raged for the previous decade. Regardless, it was only a matter of days before Cyrus Baldwin purchased Dobbs's water rights for one dollar.[293] The price seems

Cyrus G. Baldwin. *Courtesy Historical Society of Pomona Valley.*

far too reasonable, perhaps even usury, but Baldwin must have promised greater profits down the road to make Dobbs part with the valuable claims so easily and cheaply. Dobbs had a plan for diverting water into electrical utility, and Baldwin wanted to expand upon his electrical dreams; it was an ambitious partnership.

The following year, Dobbs began to cut the Falls Creek Trail along the north side of the canyon, starting at where the Mill Creek Crossing homes are now to above Big Falls on Falls Creek. He built a cabin on a flat area beyond the east bank of the creek beneath giant cedars and began to build flumes running down the north side of the canyon.[294] Remarkably, Baldwin and Dobbs intended to divert the falls by digging and blasting tunnels through the western ridge so that all of the water from Big Falls would run down the flume system, also capturing the flow of Alger Creek and Lost Creek on its way. The plan was to take the water to a penstock on the north side opposite Akers' Forest Home to a power generating plant. Baldwin, who seems to have been indefatigable, busily sought permissions from government entities and funding for his extraordinary Mill Creek project while Dobbs and company blasted and dug their way beneath what was then called Majella Falls.[295]

Best-laid plans, however, didn't take into account the possibility of drought, both financial and environmental. Despite Baldwin's prodigious gift for fundraising, which had landed him the presidency of Pomona College, the great panic of 1893, among the most serious financial setbacks

Dobbs' Cabin, circa 1900. *Courtesy Janice Gillmore private collection.*

of the nineteenth century, would last until 1897.[296] Even more damaging to Baldwin and Dobbs's endeavors was a record-breaking dry cycle that hit hard in the final two years of the century. By the time Dobbs finished the tunnels and flume line, there wasn't enough water to make the hydroelectric power generation scheme work.

Both men also had to contend with other troubles. The water shortage that was stealing the viability of Baldwin's Mill Creek project was also decimating his San Antonio Light and Power Company. Baldwin faced opposition from the Redlands power group. He was also overextended, having had to raise funds from directors for one failing power company and the purchases of extensive easements from property owners the length of Mill Creek Canyon from his own funds.[297]

Dobbs had troubles of a more personal nature. Just days before he'd filed his water claims in Mill Creek Canyon, his brother George H. Dobbs of Eureka, Kansas, murdered his neighbor in cahoots with the neighbor's wife and made national headlines.[298] George Dobbs was a widower with two children, and when he was arrested, John had to leave the work on the flume and go to Kansas to rescue his niece and nephew, Charles and Lulu Dobbs.[299] Returning with them to Redlands, Charles and Lulu were raised with John and Josephine's seven children.[300] For the next several years, the situation grew complicated, as his brother was sentenced to life in prison and declared "civilly dead." George's legal debt and property had to be dealt with on behalf of his children after George died of a brain ailment in 1904 while incarcerated.

Given the downturn in his luck, and his general overextension, it seems both curious and surprising that Baldwin would have the desire and the capital to purchase Tom Akers' Forest Home Resort. But that's what he did on March 19, 1902.[301] Unwilling to give up on his Mill Creek project, he also entered into a contract with the city of Riverside to provide power, feeling confident that he could sell the approved bond issue of $300,000 to finance it.[302] Unfortunately, the sales didn't transpire, and Baldwin lost the contract.[303] Still, his dreams weren't dimmed. On April 18, 1902, the *Evening Transcript* announced Professor Baldwin's newest idea. "He would build a cable line from his place at Forest Home to the top most peak on the summit of Mount San Bernardino. Since the Professor gave up his contract to furnish Riverside with power generated in Mill Creek canyon, he thinks he would have plenty of juice to furnish power to carry huge baskets on a cable line to and from the top of Old Grayback. Professor Baldwin thinks it would be a great and paying attraction for the festive tourist and that the summit of the lofty peak would be a favorite place for Sunday school picnics."[304]

As it happened, only tragedy could dim the ebullient Baldwin's enthusiasms. His daughter and only child, Florence, a bright, promising student at Stanford, died in a typhoid epidemic in May 1903.[305] Baldwin's basket ride never transpired, and after Florence's death, he had little to do with Forest Home resort, leaving the management to Henry Dobbs, who may have been related to John.[306] Baldwin donated 3 acres of his 160-acre Forest Home property to the Redlands YMCA for a camp named Camp Baldwin a quarter of a mile above the center of Forest Home, plus 10.5 acres to Pomona College and 10 acres to the Redlands Light and Power Company. On April 14, 1905, Baldwin sold Forest Home to the Forest Home Outing Company, which had been incorporated by his friend and fellow Congregationalist minister Frank Culver.[307] Cyrus Baldwin and his wife, Ella, moved to Palo Alto, where his life ended on January 10, 1931.[308]

John Dobbs continued to act as a guide for travelers in the mountains while he tried some prospecting and then developed land in Highland.[309] As the clock ticked over to the twentieth century, Dobbs's rustic log cabin in the forest, which harked back to a time of pioneers and mountaineers, was considered the height of picturesque and was widely featured on postcards.

Postcard, Dobbs's
Cabin, circa
1900. *Courtesy
Janice Gillmore
private collection.*

Although John Dobbs's backbreaking work to develop electrical power in
Mill Creek Canyon came to naught, in a somewhat ironic twist, his life was
in fact transformed by electricity. In July 1904, Dobbs was guiding botanist
George B. Grant and his cousin Walter Wheeler to the summit of Mount
San Gorgonio when a summer storm blew up. Charles F. Saunders relates
the story as told to him by Grant.

> *It was as black as smoke from a locomotive funnel. I never thought of
> lightning, and I don't think the others did. What we were afraid of was
> a hurricane or hailstorm. Suddenly there was a crash of thunder and a
> blinding flash. The bolt stunned the guide* [Dobbs], *and sent him plumb
> crazy, so I had to hold him by force to the ground for half an hour, or he
> would have thrown himself off the mountains. A second bolt that followed
> killed Wheeler instantly, ripping his clothes to shreds and leaving him
> almost naked. Then a third bolt struck close to me while I was struggling
> with Dobbs, who cried like a baby and was calling for his mother. I couldn't
> make him realize what had happened. Other bolts followed striking here
> and there on neighboring buttes, and there I was with a dead man and a
> lunatic on my hands and no help so far as I knew within a dozen miles, and
> the mountain wild with storm.*[310]

Josephine and John Dobbs.
Courtesy Kathy Mackrill private collection.

John W. Dobbs survived the lightning strike and lived to the age of eighty, dying in 1936.[311] But it's said that after the incident on Mount San Gorgonio, and for the rest of his life, when a thunderstorm blew up, Dobbs was a man who made himself very scarce.

THE BURRIS FAMILY

MANSIONS OF MARBLE AND A ROCKY ROAD RACE

Discovery consists of seeing what everybody has seen,
and thinking what nobody has thought.
—Albert Szent-Gyorgyi

1907—While prospecting for gold, George Burris and his sons discovered a massive wall of translucent white marble near the end of Mill Creek Canyon. The discovery created a new town and one of the most insane road races imaginable.

George Burris and Elizabeth Wallace married on Christmas Day in 1879 in Chillicothe, Missouri.[312] Both were flotsam on that great westward migration tide—he from Ohio[313] and she from Minnesota when it was still just a territory. Initially, they lived with George's family on the Burris farm in Rich Hill, Livingston County, Missouri, and they had their first child, John, named after George's father, in 1880.[314] A daughter, Georgia, followed two years later. About every two years thereafter, George and Elizabeth welcomed a new son: Charles, Oscar, Arthur and Earle, the last son born in California, where they could drift no farther west.[315]

In 1900, George was forty-four and working as a carpenter for the railroad in Los Angeles, and his eldest son, John, was working on commission as a merchant. It was a mundane start to the century for the Burris family. George seems to have been searching for something more than he had at the time, as he took two of his sons to the mountains to do a little prospecting.[316] It was a time when many prospectors were staking claims hoping to take wealth from the ground in Mill Creek Canyon.[317] Octavius Gass, onetime owner of the Las Vegas Rancho in Nevada who had been a partner with Daniel Sexton in the Temescal tin mines, was living in Mill Creek Canyon at the time, working a quartz vein that he hoped would lead to gold.[318] It wouldn't. No one had struck it rich in Mill Creek Canyon, and George Burris wouldn't make his fortune in precious metals there, either. But the canyon had another secret to reveal to him.

Exploring the north side of the valley almost to its terminus at the Mill Creek Jumpoff, the Burris men saw something that was probably seen before but was somehow not quite recognized for what it was: a massive wall of translucent white marble. Burris's find made headlines.

The recent discovery of immense deposits of marble of many different kinds in Mill Creek Cañon, about twenty miles northeast of Redlands is exciting much interest, and those who have visited the mountains where the marble is to be found are scarcely able to express their surprise at finding such rich and beautiful formations so near at hand and in quantities almost too great to be imagined. The wonder is that the marble was not discovered long ago, as Mill Creek is a much-frequented cañon and in many places the marble is plainly exposed to view. One deposit 500 feet in height and half a mile in length shows the landscape marble of exquisite beauty on which are imprinted the outlines of trees, vines, and flowers. At another point a beautiful white mottled marble is exposed for a height of more than a mile and a half running up from the base of the mountain.[319]

It wasn't gold, but at a time when building in California was wildly expansive, marble may actually have been as lucrative a discovery.[320] The deposit of stone was so large that it was thought it would employ one thousand men to quarry, cut and polish it. The family recorded a deed to the property on August 15, 1907, and by October, George and his son Charles had filed articles of incorporation with San Bernardino County as the California Marble Company, stating that they had a capitalization of $1 million.[321]

Experts in the field examined the marble and were impressed by the quality,[322] comparing it to the storied marbles of Italy and Egypt. One of the most impressive aspects of the discovery was the wide variety of colorings, from blue to green, pink with yellow onyx veins, pure translucent white and nearly black. George Burris quickly brought in a crew of eighteen men to start clearing debris and cleaning the face of the stone.[323] By autumn 1907, the California Marble Company was constructing buildings to house its workers and a company store, as well as machinery to begin quarrying the stone. In November 1908, the company filed a water appropriation for sixty inches of water out of Mill Creek to create hydroelectric power to operate drills and lights in the growing town, and Burris expanded his land claims by an additional 480 acres.[324] The quarry site featured "power drills, several heavy derricks and other modern machinery, including a tramway of 3,000 feet length and of sufficient capacity to handle mill blocks of from fifteen to eighteen tons."[325]

Perhaps the most important asset offered by the California Marble Company to travelers and residents of the canyon was the sixteen miles of completed road out of the eighteen needed to reach the quarry and transport the marble to market. The road would also prove to be an opportunity for George's sons Charles and Oscar to capitalize on a new fad that was sweeping the nation: road racing in "fast" new automobiles. For the middle two Burris boys, the California Marble Company was the beginning of their working lives.[326] Charles was vice-president and Oscar secretary and treasurer, but both functioned primarily as stock promoters, which seems to have afforded them relative comfort and social status. They were both deeply enamored of the racy new cars and, partly as a promotional scheme but mostly out of passion, they created the Burris Hill Cup Race in 1909.[327] "To provide for a perpetual hill climb contest between the Casa Loma hotel at Redlands and their mine at the head of Mill creek canyon, a distance of 20½ miles to an altitude of 9,580 feet, Charles W. and Oscar V. Burris of the California Marble company, have offered a handsome silver cup to be held by the driver of the contesting automobiles making the best time, until the record is broken by another."

This race, in quite primitive automobiles, up boulder-strewn Mill Creek Canyon, was unique and treacherous. One headline summed up the Burris Hill Cup Race as a "probably unequaled course in America for cars to go against, and hardships are severe."[328] What's more, the manner in which Charles and Oscar designed the race made it perpetual, with one driver continuously challenging another so that almost monthly someone was running the race to the quarry.[329] Drivers and their sporty new models with names like Royal Tourist, Columbia, Matheson and Stearns took up the challenge each time with hair-raising tales of their derring-do. In October

1909, a driver named Al Livingstone drove his Royal Tourist car for the cup win. The *Los Angeles Herald* reported: "Known as one of the most fearless—indeed, dare-devil-drivers on the coast, Livingstone says 'a trip over the Burris hill climb will take the heart out of any man that drives it.' It must be a terrific affair when Livingstone admits that it will make him stare at it, for it is said of him that there isn't a spot where he could work the throttle of a car that he would not take her, no matter what happened."

According to the same reporting, however, it was really Livingstone's mechanic, a fellow by the name of McDonough, who was the hero in the face of jaw-dropping obstacles.

> *When the trip of the Royal is measured up too much praise cannot be given to nervy McDonough, who was Livingstone's mechanician. Going up the hill on a good speed, climbing over rocks and boulders, McDonough was thrown out and the irons of the car caught his clothing and almost denuded the poor fellow, and the wheels of the immense car, weighing close to 2,000 pounds, came within a hair of passing over his face, but the plucky and loyal mechanician arose, ran and jumped onto his seat and said to his companion, the pegging driver Livingstone, "Never mind me keep on going and win this race."*

Livingstone's lightning-fast winning time to navigate the twenty-two-mile course from Redlands was fifty-nine minutes and forty seconds.[330] Mind you, drivers who challenged the course had to navigate 1,013 turns, cross the creek thirteen times and open and close five gates during the race as well as climb to an elevation of over nine thousand feet. Winners and their "mechanicians" were feted at Burris Camp and rewarded with a large silver cup.[331]

At the zenith of the race's popularity in 1909, a journalist mused: "Just why an automobile should be driven to the marble quarries no one knows. The road is filled with boulders. Sharp rocks bar the progress of an automobile. The drive is dangerous."[332] He wasn't the only one questioning the wisdom of racing in Mill Creek Canyon. On October 23, 1909, under the headline, "No More Racing in Mill Canyon," San Bernardino County supervisor Sid V. Horton announced that law officers had been instructed to arrest anyone racing up the canyon.[333] He had issued an edict that the racing should stop but was ignored and was reported to be in "a wrathy mood," vowing to ensure that arrests of racers were carried out. The Burris Hill Cup Race expired a short time later.

The race and its notoriety may or may not have had anything to do with the success of the California Marble Company, but the company was thriving. Not only was the marble mine in full production, the company also announced that it was building a stone mill in Los Angeles on Soto Street at the Santa Fe Railroad tracks.[334] The scale of the mill was staggering; it would be the largest stone mill west of St. Louis.[335] The central building was 112 by 150 feet and 42 feet high with 60-foot-high cranes to move blocks of marble. At the time, it was reported that the foundations had already been laid and four boxcars full of the latest stone-working equipment were en route to the site. It would also have its own private spur line on the Santa Fe Railroad 700 feet long. The scale of the Mill Creek marble deposit comes into sharp focus when it was noted that the quarry could produce columns of a single piece of marble 24 feet in length. The company intended to mill both its own stone and that of other quarries in the San Bernardino and Riverside areas. It also had a contract for a luxurious ten-story hotel at the corner of Fourth Street and Grand Avenue in downtown Los Angeles and was shipping marble to San Francisco for use in the great mansions and hotels of Nob Hill. The new town of Burris was burgeoning with all of this activity.

Although the primary residence for the Burris family was in Los Angeles, it seems that they spent considerable time at the quarry.[336] In September 1909, Elizabeth Burris, the matriarch of the family, was reported to have seen a bear while entertaining a group of lady friends at the camp.[337] The press reported that the bear "did not offer to molest" the ladies but ran off into the forest. What was unusual and newsworthy about the sighting was that bears had not been seen in that part of the range for several years, having all been hunted out.

George Burris's right to this highly productive little slice of paradise would not go unchallenged, however. The first challenge was in 1908 from three Redlands men, Joseph Ogden, H.C. Rumohr and F.G. Feraud.[338] The men claimed that they had discovered the marble deposit first and that they had gone to considerable trouble to develop the property prior to Burris. Nothing came of the situation. Later, the Southern Pacific Railroad took Burris to court, insisting that the land was within its grant.[339] In due course, officials at the United States Land Office tasked with adjudicating the suit found in favor of Burris in 1917. It was noted that he had invested more than $10,000 in improving the land and exploiting its mineral rights.[340]

Unluckily, by the 1920s, the fortunes of the California Marble Company began to crumble, quite literally. After cutting the facing stone from the

Log cabin at Burris marble quarry, 1922. *Courtesy Will H. Thrall Photograph Collection, the Huntington Library, San Marino, California.*

deposit, the inner core of the marble was extremely porous and fractured too easily to be merchantable.[341] George Burris's fast and vast investment, including developing a second plant to mill stone in Oakland, California, was unsustainable, and he sold the marble quarry property to Francis M. Townsend and Francis W. Steddom on September 22, 1925.[342] Operations at Burris Camp ground to a halt. The Mill Creek Canyon site that had been so alive grew quiet with time and lay abandoned for more than a quarter of a century.[343]

World War II would wake the sleeping marble mine again when the U.S. government needed limestone, or calcium carbonate, for armaments, bombs in particular. The quarry still had a large quantity of limestone to offer, even if the marble had given out. A man named William Ball, heading a syndicate in Los Angeles, wanted to develop the old quarry again, and Uncle Sam was behind him. It was reported that "representatives of the war production board have inspected the quarry, indicating government interest in the development." After the war, the quarry continued under the ownership of L.C. Douglas, and the site included crushers that tumbled the stone with large metal ball bearings (which people now find and mistake for cannonballs), rendering the material into a fine powder.[344] A further crushing site was built at present-day Bryant Street and California State Highway 38. But that enterprise, too, would be short-lived. By the 1950s, Burris Camp once again lay abandoned to be reclaimed by nature.

After the Mill Creek quarry was sold, the Burris family resumed their lives in Los Angeles, though they continued to have interests in mining.[345] George and Elizabeth celebrated their fiftieth anniversary with their son John at his home in Redwood City, California, in 1928. Theirs was a long, adventurous partnership. In looking back over their lives together, they may have mourned the loss of their son Arthur, who died at the age of twenty-two in 1912.[346]

The Burris family was exceptionally close. After both Charles and Oscar married, they continued to live with their parents, and over the years the siblings moved up and down the state of California and into the Reno, Nevada area more or less together.[347] Oscar and Charles continued for several years in their pursuit of motorized glory. Charles became "a professional motorcycle record breaker" for a time, doing stunts with internationally renowned cyclist Iver Lawson.[348] Oscar continued to race in his beloved Columbia motor car, which he made headlines in when he wrecked it, sending it up in flames in 1911. Later, he made a spectacular showing racing from Oakland to Los Angeles and back in twenty-eight hours and forty-five minutes.[349] Oscar worked for the Willys Overland Company and other automakers, sharing his enthusiasm in sales for several years.[350] The excitement of discovery and the bright days of the marble mine in their early lives would fade, and the Burris boys had many different careers through the course of their long lives, succumbing in their 80s, both living in the Sacramento area.[351] Their elder sister, Georgia, lived to be 101 years old,[352] and Earl, the baby of the family, lived to 91. George Burris passed away in 1942,[353] and his beloved Elizabeth followed five years later. They were 86 and 90 years old, respectively, and together they had lived the dream of the West.

D. RHEA IGO

THE EYES OF THE WORLD AND ROADSIDE ATTRACTIONS

The real secret of success is enthusiasm.
—Walter Chrysler

1911—D. Rhea Igo built a general store at the crossroads of the Mill Creek and Mountain Home Roads, where he created legends with his roadside attractions and helped to found Mountain Home Village.

During the thirty-six years that Daniel Rhea Igo lived in Mill Creek Canyon, myths and legends were born that have persisted for decades. He truly loved the canyon and contributed many lasting legacies to it with roads, resorts, a chamber of commerce, his famous general store and the unique homes that remain in Mountain Home Village, California.

Born in Bristol, Ohio, on June 18, 1887, Daniel Rhea Igo moved with his mother and father to the Mojave Desert mining town of Daggett when he was three years old and his younger brother, Benjamin, was still an infant.[354] His parents, Daniel F. Igo and Mary Elizabeth Rhea, had only been married four years when they made the move west.[355] Mary's brother, Dr. Albert R. Rhea, was the company doctor for the 20-Mule-Team Borax Company and the community of Daggett. It was the apex of the silver rush in the Calico

Mountains, and Daniel Sr., a Civil War veteran who was in his forties, tried his hand at mining. The move may have tested their marriage, however, because the Igos divorced in August 1895.[356] Life in a desert mining town as a divorced Victorian mother raising two small boys must have been challenging for Mary. Even so, she was a formidable woman, an early suffragette, who gave her sons the best life she could under the circumstances that life offered. For Daniel Rhea, the dissolution of his parents' marriage seems to have impressed a sense of responsibility on him and had a lasting effect. He chose to call himself Rhea (pronounced Ray-uh) rather than use the name he shared with his father after Daniel Sr. returned to his home state of Pennsylvania.

When Rhea was only 12, he got a job in the borax mines, working in Smith's shaft, 600 feet down in the earth pumping air into the tunnels and earning $2 a night. On one occasion the engineer, forgetting that he had a passenger in the bucket, dropped him to the bottom of the shaft with such terrific speed that he was badly shaken and bruised. He decided then that he would never be a miner. Upon the death of Calico, in 1898, his family moved to Barstow where his uncle started the first drug store. Too many saloons made it a bad environment for the two boys, so his mother decided to move to Redlands.[357]

After they were established, Mary did what genteel women often did in difficult life situations to earn money: she took in boarders at their home on East Citrus Avenue in Redlands.[358] Rhea was almost thirteen, the man of the family, and he took a job selling newspapers for the N.L. Levering

From left: D. Rhea Igo, Mary Igo and Benjamin Igo, circa 1900. *Courtesy Linda C. Driscoll, Rhea family collection.*

Times Newspaper Agency then learned to be a printer with Scipio Craig at the *Citrograph* newspaper in Redlands. One gets the sense that young Rhea was sometimes torn between having to care for his mother and brother and his own passions. He stayed with the newspaper trade, working for the *San Bernardino Sun* after the *Citrograph* closed following Craig's death in 1908. On May 4, 1910, Rhea married Maude Wilkins, a girl visiting Redlands with her family from Ohio.[359] At the age of twenty-three, he would at last find some freedom and strike off on a less conventional path.

THE CALL OF THE MOUNTAINS

During the summer of 1911, Rhea and Maude moved to Forest Home Resort. Rhea was an accomplished musician, and by night he played with other musicians for dances and spent his days guiding groups to Old Grayback. Reverend Frank J. Culver and the Forest Home Outing Company owned the resort, a popular mountain vacation spot. Despite the sheen of elegant Victorian social life, Forest Home was still fairly primitive. Culver employed a full-time trapper, Joe Razk, to keep down the number of varmints that might pester guests. Trapper Joe's death toll was regularly reported by the newspapers. At one time, his high score was twenty foxes, thirteen bobcats, forty skunks and three mountain lions (it would have been four if one lion hadn't carried off his largest trap attached to a tree four inches in diameter).[360] Trout from Mill Creek was so plentiful that one gentleman pulled in forty-three before breakfast on a Monday morning.[361]

The Igos' first cottage in the meadow at Tyler Ranch, 1918. *Courtesy Southern California Edison Collection.*

This was the world that Rhea and Maude Igo chose, and it apparently agreed with them, because they stayed in the canyon after the summer season. In the fall, they moved to the old Tyler Ranch, which was then in the control of the Covington family, where they tended the hogs and cattle. There, they leased a lovely spot near the orchards and the creek and built a little cottage to live in. There was little development in the canyon when the Igos settled there save the Edison company houses and flume, the Jacksons, Kate Harvey's house and a few cabins.

ROADS AND THE MILL CREEK PRISON CAMP

Just prior to the Igos' arrival in Mill Creek Canyon, resort owners and politicians began to envision a fine new road into the mountains. Discussions with the county board of supervisors had been quietly ongoing for some time. F.J. Culver, the owner of Forest Home Resort, started the process on his own in 1910 by building a road up the canyon for his guests. It was thought that the road would eventually integrate with the much longer and higher road into the mountains toward Seven Oaks and Bear Valley.[362] The new thoroughfare represented significant economic advantages in tourism dollars. The people of Highland wanted it to go through their city and up Santa Ana Canyon, while Redlands business interests wanted the road to pass through their town and up Mill Creek Canyon. In March 1912, at the Elks Lodge, Redlands men were riled. A speech by the owner of one of the local funeral homes called on the men to "not only contribute coin of the realm but…actually go in person and in khaki to swing the pick and shovel."[363]

That is, in fact, what the Redlands men did, with Rhea Igo leading the charge. Granted, it was a bit of a publicity stunt, but it demonstrated to the board of supervisors that both Igo and Redlands meant business. Igo had enthusiastically embraced the road-building vision doing canyon road work in 1912, which partially sustained him and Maude with county payroll.[364] Igo's brother, Ben, was a road surveyor for both the Mountain Home Canyon road and the Mill Creek road.[365] The following year, Igo became the fifth district road commissioner for the county and would serve in that position for eight years over the long—and often tortuous—building of the Mill Creek road and the road to Barton Flats.

During that long process, his neighbors were inmates of a county prison camp initially set up in the Jackson meadows. To cut costs on prison labor

Redlands businessmen's road-building stunt. *Courtesy Archives, A.K. Smiley Public Library.*

on the county rock pile, the supervisors decided to place misdemeanor miscreants in the camp in Mill Creek Canyon to work on the road.[366] The prison camp was controversial, and there were frequent shenanigans there, especially as Captain Covington (a cousin of County Supervisor Sid Horton), who was in charge of the camp, liked his booze. Covington regularly brought it into camp for "the boys." When they got liquored up, things went a little crazy.[367] The prison camp, which eventually moved closer to Thurman Flats, was seasonal, but it wasn't short-lived and remained in the canyon for more than a decade as road building progressed well into the 1920s.[368] Among the events that made headlines were riots there over grub that even the camp dogs wouldn't eat,[369] daring escapes, shocking goings-on with a form of torture called "turpentining" and even a crazy story about a man thought to have been murdered who turned up there.

NEW DEVELOPMENTS

During those years, Rhea and Maude Igo had their own new developments. On June 24, 1912, they welcomed their firstborn, a daughter named Dorothy June. On March 28, 1914, their second daughter, Maxine Rhea,

Igo's store, 1916. *Courtesy Igo family private collection.*

joined the family. Mary Igo, Rhea's mother, moved to Mill Creek Canyon to live with her son's family in 1914. The following year, Igo began to build his famous general store at the crossroads of Mill Creek and Mountain Home Creek roads. It was a well-considered idea, as it was near Kate Harvey's control, which was where travelers had to camp while waiting to use the toll road, and the store also provided a waystation on the route to Forest Home Resort. Neighboring the store was George Humphrey's Kamp Kill Kare, which made it convenient for guests staying there, too. Unquestionably, Mill Creek Canyon resorts were coming into their own as more and more travelers acquired automobiles. Igo was set to capitalize on the rollicking mountain tourism.

Mary Igo, Rhea's mother, had been very clever as a real estate investor in Redlands. In 1919, seeing an opportunity, she patented twenty acres of homestead land roughly where the Igos had built their cottage by the creek, thus securing the land for Rhea's little family.[370] The homestead was a long, narrow strip of meadow, *cienega* and orchards lined with willows along the creek. It would also become the setting of the canyon's most enduring myth.

THE MYTH

Harold Bell Wright was the first American author to sell a million copies of his books and to earn $1 million from them.[371] An ordained minister of the Disciples of Christ, Wright arrived in Redlands, California, in 1907 to be the minister at the First Christian Church on East Olive Avenue.[372] He had already authored one novel and would publish a second, *The Shepherd of the Hills,* during his year in Redlands—a year that launched his literary career and convinced him to leave the clergy. Wright chose to set a subsequent novel, *The Eyes of the World,* in Mill Creek Canyon. The novel is a very thinly veiled indictment of the social excesses in wealthy Redlands at the time, though he chose to call the town Fairlands in the book. Wright disguised elements of Mill Creek Canyon, too, calling it Clear Creek Canyon, though he named Mounts San Bernardino and San Gorgonio.[373] The story describes many features of the canyon that are readily identifiable, such as the "gates" at the entrance, the pipeline trail, the area around Mountain Home Creek and Mill Creek, the old ranger station and well-known trails. Wright is said to have camped in the canyon after moving to Redlands, but his autobiography and letters don't leave many specific clues as to when or for how long, or anyone he may have met or known while spending time by Mill Creek.

The Eyes of the World became Wright's most popular novel, selling more than 750,000 copies and inspiring two film versions of the story, one in 1916 and another in 1930.[374] The first, a silent feature produced by the Clune Motion Picture Company and directed by Donald Crisp[375] (who later won a Best Supporting Actor Oscar for his role in the film *How Green Was My Valley*), was filmed in Mill Creek Canyon in 1916. Harold Bell Wright was very much involved in that production. Rhea Igo is said to have acted as location scout. He also claimed that Wright modeled characters in the novel named Carleton after him and Maude. Later, Igo created a roadside attraction proclaiming that Harold Bell Wright had written his novel in a small cabin built for the silent film that was left by the Clune

Harold Bell Wright, America's first millionaire author. *Courtesy Library of Congress.*

Rhea Igo's roadside attraction billboard. *Courtesy Igo family private collection.*

Movie set cabin from the 1916 silent film *The Eyes of the World. Courtesy Archives, A.K. Smiley Public Library.*

Company on his property. In fact, Wright wrote *The Eyes of the World* at his Imperial Valley ranch called Tecolote, near El Centro, where he and his family moved in 1908.[376] Regardless, the story and the fame of Harold Bell Wright brought people to the Igos' store and ranch. Igo attempted to subdivide his land in the big meadow along the creek, calling it the Eyes of the World Ranch, but he was unsuccessful, because he couldn't secure water rights.[377] Even so, the long straightaway along the open meadow above Mountain Home Village on California State Highway 38 is still called Eyes of the World by locals.

MILL CREEK CANYON PARK

Mary Igo passed away on December 22, 1924, leaving considerable property to Rhea and Ben. Four months later, George Humphrey, the owner of Kamp Kill Kare, purchased thirty-six acres from Southern California Edison contiguous to his property to develop as a subdivision with ninety-six lots called Mill Creek Canyon Park.[378] Kenneth Bright and his wife, Louise, had purchased the old Tyler ranch and partnered with Humphrey and Igo in this new venture. Rhea Igo was the sales agent selling out of a tiny stone building that still exists, and he sold eleven lots on the first day at a cost of $200 each. By the following summer, lot owners were busily constructing homes and Igo had succeeded in selling forty-three of the ninety-six lots. Ultimately, just after the stock market crash of 1929, Humphrey and Igo sold their two-thirds interest in Mill Creek Canyon Park for $50,000. The deal allowed Igo to retain his store and filling station, which were on the same property.[379]

Rhea Igo was a beloved figure who contributed a great deal to Mill Creek Canyon. He had the first school bus service, taking kids to school in Redlands, and he was instrumental in founding the Mill Creek Canyon Chamber of Commerce in the 1930s, which sponsored events and lobbied for a new highway to Barton Flats and Big Bear, which is now a portion of State Highway 38.[380] Most memorable is Igo's store featuring a soda fountain that was a popular stop for ice cream in the summer on trips to the mountains. The store had a comfortable old-time atmosphere that invited people to sit a while on the porch and visit. Moreover, Igo and his family were always there for their community in times of need. In 1937, when a cabin in the Falls Tract several miles away caved in, trapping three families and killing

Maude and Rhea Igo and visitors. *Courtesy Igo family private collection.*

Rhea Igo with grandchildren Diane Bandy and "Pat" Bandy behind them. *Courtesy Igo family private collection.*

D. Rhea Igo, circa 1940s. *Courtesy Igo family private collection.*

one man, twenty-four-year-old Dorothy Igo drove a snow plow the length of the canyon in heavy snows to lead rescuers to the victims.[381] During the catastrophic flood of 1938 that washed away the ranger station and several homes and cabins, the Igos took in families who had lost everything in the floodwaters.[382]

Sadly, Igo's years of service to Mill Creek Canyon were cut short. While on a train on his way to comfort his brother Ben, whose wife, Gladys, had just passed away, Rhea suffered a heart attack and died on November 26, 1947. He was sixty years old.[383]

The Igo family and their store were so synonymous with the area that the Mill Creek Canyon Park subdivision became known to everyone as Igo's. It remained the de facto name of the community for decades until residents petitioned the county board of supervisors to give their community an official name. They chose Mountain Home Village. The supervisors gave the name their blessing on June 29, 1964. It was the end of an era, and the newspaper announcement was headlined, "No Longer Igo's."[384]

Maude and her daughters, Dorothy and Maxine, with the help of their children, continued to run the store and soda fountain until 1958, when they sold it to Jackson and Priscila Titus. It continues to be called Igo's store to this day, even though it is now a private residence.

13

LOUIE E. TORREY

FARMING THE FOREST AND A NOTORIOUS TAVERN

It is not so much for its beauty that the forest makes a claim upon men's hearts, as for that subtle something, that quality of air that emanation from old trees, that so wonderfully changes and renews a weary spirit.
—*Robert Louis Stevenson*

1911—Louie and Margaret Torrey had a farm on the north side of Mill Creek that grew into Torrey's resort, a popular destination for families. They also owned Torrey's Tavern and its pool and campground.

Louie Ellsworth Torrey's life began on May 15, 1865, in Saratoga, Illinois, among farmers.[385] His father, Charles W. Torrey, and mother, Frances G. Pierce, moved their family to Sheridan, Kansas, on the Kansas/Missouri line, when Louie was about two years old in 1867.[386] He grew up farming with his father as the only son with just one sister, Minnie, who was ten years his junior.[387] Charles Torrey had a large family, and throughout Louie's childhood at least two of his uncles and their families came to live nearby in Prescott, Kansas, including Joseph H. Torrey and Chauncey B. Torrey.[388]

Joe Torrey and his wife, Carrie, had three daughters when they lost their little daughter, Ethel, who was fifteen months old in January 1887.[389] They would soon lose another baby girl, Florence Cecil, to diphtheria in 1890. Joe went to California and bought a large ranch in Wilmington, near

Louie Torrey's father, Charles W. Torrey, and his family. *Standing from left*: Charles, Eliza, Martha, Ellen and Edward. *Seated from left*: Chauncy, Nicholas, Ira and Melissa Torrey (Louie's grandparents) and Joseph. *Courtesy Torrey family private collection.*

Long Beach. When he moved his family west, he took his twenty-two-year-old nephew Louie with him to help get a dairy business started.[390] Louie apparently liked California, but his heart was in Kansas with Margaret "Maggie" Miller, a popular girl back home.[391] Louie returned to his hometown to marry Maggie on December 1, 1892, in Prescott, Kansas.[392] He was twenty-seven and Maggie twenty-two. Within a couple of weeks, the Torreys were on the move west again, and their send-off demonstrates how well loved they were. "Joe Torrey and family, Chauncey Torrey and family, Louie Torrey and his young wife started for California Monday. Mr. and Mrs. Chauncey Torrey leave a large circle of friends who greatly regret their departure. Louie Torrey, having late returned from California and married one of our fair ladies, makes for himself and wife a new home in the golden state leaving a vacant place in our midst which is not easily filled. We wish for all of them a realization of their bright hopes."[393]

The future seemed very bright indeed for Louie and Maggie and the westward-bound Torrey family. Louie and Maggie settled in the Clearwater area and in 1894 had their first son, Louie Ellsworth Torrey Jr., who would be called Ellsworth throughout his life. Two years later, on January 4, 1896, a second son was born, Charles Elijah Torrey.

Between 1902 and 1910, Long Beach, California, was the fastest-growing city in America.[394] Louie Torrey had a sharp eye for business, and he started the Long Beach Transfer and Warehouse Company, a moving and storage business capitalizing on the influx of migrants. Torrey had the first auto truck in Long Beach for his business, but the newfangled automobiles proved to be troublesome.[395] On September 15, 1909, it was reported, "The new auto truck of the Long Beach Transfer company has already figured in its first accident, when it pushed its front end into a vegetable wagon, scattering farm produce generously along Pine avenue."[396] The scene seems slapstick, but two years later, it was no laughing matter when an automobile tragedy struck Louie Torrey in earnest.[397]

> *An auto truck owned by the Long Beach Transfer Company was run into and overturned by a short line Pasadena car [train] last night on Huntington Drive. W.E. English and L.E. Torrey, who had charge of the truck were caught underneath the big vehicle and badly injured. Torrey's arms and shoulders were mashed and it is feared that English has sustained serious injury to the spine. The truck, which had broken down, was being towed by an automobile. The chauffer of the latter saw the flagman at the crossing and saw the approaching car [train], but as he was hauled up on the tracks, he tried to make it across.[398]*

Louie Torrey was forty-six, and his injuries were severe. It was going to take time and rest to heal. During his long recuperation, the Torreys took vacations to Forest Home Resort. When Louie was sufficiently recovered, he engaged in real estate in Long Beach, selling off lots in the Torrey Tract,[399] leaving the work of the moving company to manager J.W. Rogers and the bookkeeping to Ellsworth, who had graduated high school and come into the business. In 1915, perhaps longing for a simpler life, the Torreys left their comfortable living in Long Beach and homesteaded on the north side of Mill Creek Canyon across the creek from Forest Home.

Living like pioneers, they created a real farm in Mill Creek Canyon. It was no small job. The land was rocky, and up in the part that Louie wanted to farm, it was covered in unforgiving manzanita and brush. Whatever they had they grew or made themselves. They cultivated their own food; hauled water; grew crops; planted orchards of apple, cherry and peach trees from present-day Lakeview at Forest Home to Inspiration Point; and grew corn on the flat areas. Louie invented a pulley system to haul corn down the hill, and in light of the injuries to his arms and shoulders, he had to be ingenious to accomplish many of the hard tasks of farming.

The Torreys' son, Charley, was nineteen when they moved to their canyon homestead. During one of the family's vacations at Forest Home, he'd sparked up a summer romance with Phillis Hird, the daughter of J.P. Hird, proprietor of Redlands' Alvarado Hotel. As the United States became involved in the war in Europe and Charley went into the army, this romance became serious. On June 3, 1917, Phillis and Charley were married at sunrise atop Mount Rubidoux in Riverside.[400] Phillis moved in with Louie and Margaret at their farm while Charley was in Company C, Los Angeles, in Victorville. On August 8, 1918, he shipped out on the *Mentor* from Brooklyn, New York, bound for France.[401] Phillis gave birth to their first child, a daughter named Margaret Clark Torrey, just two days later.[402] Phillis may have been a comfort and help, but Louie and Margaret had lost the physical strength of their son. Ellsworth, for unknown reasons, didn't serve in the war and preferred to live in the city working as a bookkeeper and office manager for different firms in Long Beach and Los Angeles.[403] He was also embarking on a matrimonial path that would include four marriages between 1919 and 1952.[404] Meanwhile, Charley was fighting in the deadliest battle in American history, the Meuse-Argonne offensive in France, fought between September 26 and November 11, 1918.[405] More than 26,000 American soldiers perished, but Charley, fortunately, was one who came home, on April 12, 1919, with Phillis waiting for his train to arrive in Los Angeles.[406] In the mountains, Torrey's camp was a verdant wilderness with a garden filled with fresh vegetables and orchards fragrant with fruit, the sound of the creek filling the silence beneath the trees. One can only imagine how Charley felt returning to Mill Creek Canyon and his young wife and parents after witnessing wholesale slaughter in France.

For the first few years of their residency, the Torreys lived in a tiny stone homestead cabin built by an erstwhile homesteader named Van Zandt that is still at Creekside at Forest Home. They finally built a larger stone home in 1919,* which is still there, and another cabin for Charley and Phillis to live in.[407] Soon, they added more cabins for friends to stay in when they visited. Before long, their farm became a camp and was thereafter known as Torrey's Camp.[408] What's interesting is that, unlike all of the other resorts in the area,

---

* For decades, the Torreys' home was the dining room for the Lost Creek Ranch or Camp Rancho, as Creekside was known.

they scarcely advertised; people just came by word of mouth. Over the years following the war, Charley's love for nature and animals became evident as he collected a peculiar assortment of critters, which were exhibited as a petting zoo. These included horses and burros for guests to ride, the usual farm animals such as cows and chickens and more exotic offerings such as a monkey, a tame bobcat and even an elk for a period of time.

By the time the Torreys began to have paying guests, Forest Home Resort directly across Mill Creek was under the management of Frank Culver Jr., the son of Reverend Frank Culver, who had purchased it from Cyrus Baldwin then subsequently retired.[409] Under the management of the Culvers, Forest Home had added improvements, including nicely furnished cabins with hot baths and showers, a new dining room and a dance pavilion.[410] During that period, Forest Home became popular with a much wealthier and racier set. This was especially so in the 1920s, when the Jazz Age settled in to stay and jazz babies flocked to Forest Home to the new dance pavilion to dance to Wade Hamilton's Marimbaphone Jazz Orchestra. A somewhat sniffy article in the *Los Angeles Times* made clear the sort of guests the resort courted, characterizing Forest Home as the "most accessible and popular of high mountain resorts for real folks of the better class." Torrey's, however, was a resort for families and just plain folks. Louie Torrey added a swimming pool near the front gate and croquet and badminton courts. Trails with bridges over springs in the forest meandered beneath the trees around their property, and the establishment's devoted guests returned year after year. Margaret Torrey was known for her hospitality and the unusual handicrafts she made and sold, such as pine needle baskets, and her cooking was greatly admired. Both Louie and Margaret felt strongly about the idea of community, and they invited their neighbors and friends to freely pick fruit from their orchards and kept canyon residents and visitors supplied with corn, fresh vegetables, eggs, milk and cream for sale.

The land confusion prevailing in Mill Creek Canyon at the time with the U.S. government, the railroads and power companies claiming title to land meant that the Torreys didn't have any legal right to the property they had been farming for almost seven years, until they finally received a homestead patent in 1921. The land conveyed by the U.S. government, however, was far less than they'd been using—only 62 6/100 acres.[411] On June 21, 1921, Louie Torrey purchased the rest of the land that he wanted plus a portion of another section on December 20, 1923, from the Southern Sierras Power Company.[412] These purchases secured not only the farming land and orchards that Louie and his family had already cleared, planted

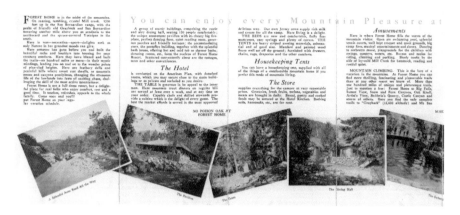

Frank Culver's Forest Home Resort, circa 1916. *Courtesy Archives, A.K. Smiley Public Library, Redlands, California.*

and built on, but also considerably more land on which to develop other paying concerns. The hardworking Torreys were putting down deep roots in Mill Creek Canyon.

Charley's wife, Phillis, was expecting another child, and living in such a remote location may have been a concern. They moved to Redlands and on January 19, 1923, welcomed a son, Charles Philip Torrey.[413] Despite their joy in their two young children, a darkness was descending on Charley. Both he and his brother Ellsworth suffered from a rare genetic disease of the arteries and veins called Buerger's disease that affects the extremities and is exacerbated by tobacco use.[414] Over time, it causes the loss of circulation to limbs and results in gangrene and amputation.[415] Charley lost first one foot, then the other, and then his lower legs, leaving him wheelchair-bound for the rest of his life. It didn't slow him down one bit, but his marriage didn't last, and he came back to live in the mountains with his parents.[416]

Louie and Margaret enjoyed sharing their success with their community. On October 14, 1931, they deeded some of their land to the newly formed Fallsvale School District for the price of $150 to build the first permanent school for the children of Mill Creek Canyon.[417] Master stonemason Martin Fagerstedt and a crew of locals built the beautiful new one-room schoolhouse out of Mill Creek stone over the course of several months. Fallsvale School opened for its first class on September 12, 1932, with Edna Johnson as the teacher.[418] In 1934, Johnson was replaced by Helen Logan, who would stay for many, many years.

Wallace "Wallie" Fagerstedt, the stonemason's son, lived at what was then called Igo's, now Mountain Home Village, and Logan stopped in her Model

T Ford for Wallie and his friend Bob Clark to take them to the schoolhouse each school day morning. On Wallie's eleventh birthday, March 2, 1938, a stupendous storm erupted over the mountains. Mill Creek Canyon is steep and relatively narrow, with Mill Creek running down its center. The water from dozens of other creeks and washes funnels down from the ridges on either side, swelling the main channel many feet high and rushing down the length of the canyon, carrying trees and rocks with it. Even at the age of eighty-nine, Wallie's memories of that day were very vivid.

> *It rained terrible, and I mean it really rained. The water had to be at least four or five hundred feet across and twenty feet deep and it was moving. They estimate that it was doing 70 miles per hour when it left the canyon. Mrs. Logan said we've got to close down school and go home. So, she jumped in her car and she took Bob and me and we got down to where there used to be a bridge from* [the stone house on the main road called] *Point Breeze to where the Edison intake is, there was a bridge that went clear across. When we started to cross that bridge it was swaying and just when we got across, the whole thing collapsed. I don't know what ever possessed that woman to go across that bridge! It scared Bob and me to death! And then when we got down to the Y* [the turnoff from Forest Falls to State Highway 38], *the water was almost to the windows of the car coming out of Monkeyface Falls and we went through that. It was a scary ride, but she made it out of the canyon. When I got home, there was my birthday cake on the table and the flood was so bad there it sat for days. There was a brand-new house right* [down the road from our house] *and I saw it go off and it floated like an ark as far as we could see then broke up, it was that much water and of course the ground was shaking. It was terrible. I think it was 67 houses were lost in the canyon.*[419]

Torrey's Camp was particularly hard hit because of its proximity to the creek. N.L. Levering reported: "Torrey's is wiped out. Dozens of cabins are gone."[420] Worse, two people died trying to cross Mill Creek.[421] It was a devastating time for the residents of the canyon, but Torrey's Camp was on the relatively uninhabited side and was cut off. Louie was then seventy-two and Margaret sixty-eight. Charley, unable to get to them, must have been frantic. All of the resort owners in Mill Creek Canyon suffered losses.[422]

Frank Culver Jr. at Forest Home had gotten into a pickle with debt and couldn't cover the losses of the flood. The resort was purchased by investors and became the property of Harold Durant of Redlands.[423] Durant had little interest in running a resort, especially one that had become a little down at the heels and fraught with flood damage. He decided to cut his losses and sell Forest Home to a nondenominational religious organization headed by Henrietta Mears, but the steadfast Torreys rebuilt and carried on.[424]

Prior to 1938, Louie had built a second resort a short distance up the canyon with a tavern restaurant called Torrey's Tavern, a swimming pool, cabins and a campground that Charley lived at and managed. Louie and Charley applied to the state for a liquor license for the tavern in 1938, but opponents argued that the license would be detrimental to the new religious camp at Forest Home as well as young vacationers and that the tavern was too close to Fallsvale school.[425] Charley defended his project in the press, arguing that the tavern was six hundred feet from the school and that three of the four Fallsvale school board members welcomed the tavern. He stated: "We propose to operate it as a high-class institution that would give no cause for protest. Other liquor licenses in the canyon have already been granted." The state agreed with the opponents and denied the license.[426] Despite that ruling and the opposition, or perhaps because of it, Torrey's Tavern developed a vaguely underground character. It was the popular spot for the younger crowd, with live music and a great dance floor.[427] People brought their own beverages in brown paper bags, and Charley turned a blind eye.[428] In the summer months, he rolled across the road in his wheelchair from the tavern to the pool before it opened in the morning and tossed pockets full of silver dollars into the water for the kids to dive for.[429] There was an interesting underside to Charley's largesse, however; he had illegal slot machines in the tavern, and the silver dollars were ill-gotten gains. He would eventually run afoul of the law and be arrested, his slot machines confiscated, but he was quickly released with a $250 fine and carried on.[430]

In the 1940s, Louie and Margaret opened a little café in Redlands on West State Street called Torrey's Frosty Lane.[431] Charley's son, Phil, worked there, as did Billie Frances Smith, a Redlands girl whom Phil would later marry.[432] In 1941, Phil enlisted in the U.S. Marines and went to fight in World War II in the Pacific,[433] while his dad, Charley, headed up a squad of civilian plane spotters watching for enemy aircraft in Mill Creek Canyon. At eighty-two and seventy-seven, respectively, Louie and Margaret finally decided to retire, and they sold their original Torrey's Camp acreage to Forest Home Christian Conference Center across the creek in 1947 and then moved to Redlands. They kept Torrey's Tavern so that Charley would continue to have a livelihood—but as it turned out, not for long.

Charley Torrey at Torrey's Tavern with Guard, his constant companion, circa 1945. *Courtesy Gina Swank Prather private collection.*

On April 11, 1954, Charley Torrey lost his battle with Buerger's disease at the age of fifty-eight.[434] His brother, Ellsworth, made certain that Charley had a veteran's headstone, and he moved to Redlands to be near his elderly parents after Charley's death. Ellsworth lived for only a year before he, too, succumbed to Buerger's disease on November 2, 1956.[435] He was sixty-three. Margaret Torrey at the age of eighty-seven followed her boys into death on July 11, 1957.[436] Louie Torrey, the adventurous boy who left Kansas for a bright new start in California, was predeceased by all those he loved most. The long, pioneering trail finally ended for Louie on October 15, 1959. He was ninety-four years old.[437]

Louie and Maggie Torrey's legacy lives on in Mill Creek Canyon in the stone buildings they built at Creekside at Forest Home, the name of Torrey Pines Road, the old Fallsvale Schoolhouse and Torrey's Tavern, which had many other lives after Charley Torrey's death. These incarnations included the Sip 'n Dip and Valley of the Falls Community Church. It is now the Forest Falls Seventh-day Adventist Church.

14

NOAH L. LEVERING

THE VALLEY OF THE FALLS AND THE BIRTH OF A COMMUNITY

All growth depends upon activity. There is no development physically or
intellectually without effort, and effort means work.
—Calvin Coolidge

1920—Banker Noah L. Levering purchased a 640-
acre section of land at the top of Mill Creek Canyon
from the Southern Pacific Railroad, which he
developed as the Valley of the Falls Tract with home
and business lots for sale.

Noah Lee Levering was a different kind of pioneer. Best described as
a capitalist citizen prince, he was a member of the generation that
was one step away from America's early agrarian culture and forging ahead
into the Industrial Age. Levering seems to have inherited the essential
restlessness and ambition of his father, Noah Levering. Noah Levering the
elder was born to a well-heeled family in Ohio in 1827 and studied law
with Abraham Lincoln's law partner in Illinois. He was said to have ridden
the circuit with Lincoln himself,[438] and he had the sixteenth president as
a reference on his professional cards for a number of years. Assuredly, he
was peripatetic, breaking new professional ground while pushing westward.
Noah Levering married Margaret Fry Martin in Springfield, Illinois, in 1855
then took her and their ever-increasing family to Iowa, Missouri and finally

Young Noah L. Levering. *Courtesy Archives, A.K. Smiley Public Library, Redlands, California.*

California, where he founded the Southern California Historical Society and became an apiarist.[439] "By 1875, when Levering made his last change of residence, this time to Los Angeles, he had made a 'career of careers.' He had been a school teacher, lawyer, city clerk, county judge, officer in the military, and chief of a draft board. He had also been a merchant and a postmaster."[440]

Noah Levering the younger, known as Lee, was born in Mecklin, Missouri, on March 28, 1869, during his father's tenure in the dry goods business and as postmaster.[441] Lee was the fourth of the Leverings' five children and was six years old when they came to California.[442] As a boy of fourteen in 1883, he tied his fortunes to the new *Los Angeles Times* newspaper. He recalled: "Four other boys and I delivered all the papers The Times published....Then I worked in the circulation department, then in the advertising department and the editorial department, in fact did everything but write editorials."[443]

While still working for the *Times*, he earned a degree in 1890 from the Los Angeles State Normal School, which eventually became the University of California, Los Angeles.[444] Lee became a grammar-school teacher in 1892, teaching primarily in Los Angeles schools. He was also dabbling in real estate, acting as a private mortgage lender, and he and his younger brother, Martin, owned interests in the fruit-farming business in Ventura.[445] Like his father, one career couldn't satisfy N.L. Levering.

Lee Levering and Ella May Gird may have been acquainted with one another prior to a New Year's Eve party in 1893, but a romance seems to have blossomed from that moment. Levering worked courtship into his extremely busy life, and on October 2, 1895, at the age of twenty-six, he married May, as she was known, at her parents' home in a quiet ceremony with little fanfare.[446] May's family were very prominent landowners in Southern California. Her father, Edward Kinsley Gird, and his brother Henry had come overland to California, driving ox teams in 1853 and tried farming in Northern California for five years. Edward returned to Illinois to marry Lucy Dew Lewis then moved to Missouri, where May and her siblings were born. In 1868, the family came to California and purchased

80 acres for a dairy farm. Their farmhouse would eventually be in the center of the Wilshire District in Los Angeles. Henry Gird, Ella May's uncle, owned the 1,000-acre La Cienega Rancho, including the renowned La Brea Tar Pits and much of the present Wilshire District. Moreover, Richard Gird, a cousin, founded the town of Tombstone, Arizona, and made a fortune in silver and copper mines. He purchased the 42,000-acre Chino Rancho (once owned by Colonel Isaac Williams, who purchased the first sawmill in Mill Creek Canyon from Daniel Sexton) and began the sugar beet industry in California on the rancho, which became the town of Chino, California. Lee Levering had married well, and they soon had a daughter, Lucy, born in 1897.

In 1899, Lee and May moved to Redlands, California.[447] There, Levering went into partnership with his brother-in-law Philip Royar (married to his older sister Mamie)[448] in the Redlands News and Stationery Company and continued his relationship with the *Los Angeles Times* as a news agent. Redlands in 1900, where the millionaire elites of the East wintered, was just the place for an ambitious young married couple with good social graces.[449] Both were involved with the robust social and service clubs in the city.

A son, Lee Gird, who went by Gird, was born in 1901. Within a few years, delightful social-column stories of the period offered insights into Levering's status and his children's seemingly magical lives. One especially imaginative entertainment held at their home on Pearl Avenue in Redlands was an elaborately staged fairy tale. "Hundreds of Redlands persons doffed the workaday clothes of life Friday evening and gathered in 'The Witch's Orchard,' which happens to be a part of the beautiful estate of N.L. Levering on The Terrace, to see 'The Rescue of the Princess Winsome.' It was an outdoor affair, the stage being between two great cypress trees, around one of which the Ogre's tower was built, with a background of matted shrubs. The garden was decorated with witch lanterns."

In 1902, the *Los Angeles Times* noted: "N.L. Levering and his brother-in-law E.C. Gird, who is news agent at the Soldiers' Home [Sawtelle Veterans' Home], accompanied by their families, started up into the mountains yesterday on a camping expedition. They will be on the upper Mill Creek Cañon, a little below the falls."

That year, the Leverings and Girds stayed in the mountains for almost six weeks and took their milk cow with them.[450] It became an annual pilgrimage to Pine Flat, a surprisingly remote location in the upper canyon well beyond Forest Home, which was itself still just a primitive camp.[451]

From left: Edward C. Gird, Mary Gird and Ella May Gird, circa 1880. *Courtesy Janice Gillmore private collection.*

In 1904, the Leverings had another daughter, Vivian, and Philip Royar sold his interest in the stationery and news agency business to Levering, because he was suffering ill health. Soon, Lee was in a partnership with H.H. Lienau and R. Holtby Myers in the Highway Construction Company, a road-building and -paving business. Their first big job was paving Cajon Street in Redlands. Levering changed careers again when he sold the

Above: The Leverings coming up the canyon in their wagon. *Courtesy Janice Gillmore private collection.*

Left: Frances Gird on horseback in Mill Creek Canyon, circa 1900. *Courtesy Janice Gillmore private collection.*

The Girds and Leverings camping at Pine Flat, circa 1900. *Courtesy Janice Gillmore private collection.*

The Girds dining beneath the pines, circa 1900. *Courtesy Janice Gillmore private collection.*

stationery business to C.W. Craig in June 1910 with an inventory of $10,000 that he had built from an investment of $25.[452] He kept his interest in the paving company, but his new venture was the takeover of the First Bank of Highland, purchasing controlling interest and embarking on a new career as a banker with his brother Martin. He was forty-one.

The year 1920 would place Levering permanently on the map of Mill Creek Canyon. The Levering brothers sold the majority interest they'd acquired in the San Bernardino Savings Bank to three eastern bankers, and Lee had cash to invest. On November 16, 1920, the *San Bernardino County Sun* newspaper headlined Levering's next move: "Big Deal in Mountain Land."[453]

One of the biggest deals in local mountain lands that has been consummated in many months is that just announced by N.L. Levering whereby he acquires section 17 from the Southern Pacific Railroad Company. Mr. Levering states that he will at once improve his new holding and place it upon the market in homesite lots. Although his plans are not fully matured, Mr. Levering stated…that he will have a new road, possibly of concrete, constructed from Forest Home to his property. Survey for this is to be made immediately. He plans to bring domestic water from a spring on the southern portion of his holdings, piping it to each lot. He will make the water system a mutual concern, with each lot owner having one share in the company. Plans are also maturing whereby electricity may be supplied each lot, probably on the same basis. This section is strategically located along resort lines and Mr. Levering plans to make it one of the finest in the mountains hereabouts.

Levering had purchased the last of the railroad sections in Mill Creek Canyon, 640 acres, or one square mile, taking control of the largest undeveloped land. It encompassed everything from the west end of present Oak and Pine Streets to Big Falls on both sides of the canyon, all unoccupied land with the exception of Burris Camp, which was swiftly winding down and would soon be abandoned.[454] Levering had a vision for this vast sweep of mountain land: to create a new community called Valley of the Falls with homes and businesses, particularly resorts. However, bringing this vision to fruition in a remote wilderness was a colossal job. Levering sold land above Forest Home to the Southern Sierras Power Company for a power plant, but water had to be diverted to develop the hydroelectric power above the Southern California Edison Company's infrastructure in much the same way proposed earlier by Cyrus G. Baldwin.[455] There was also no real road

Chester Gillmore, husband of Maybelle Gird. *Courtesy Janice Gillmore private collection.*

beyond Forest Home except the rocky dirt road to the quarry, which had enticed road racers but wouldn't accommodate families in automobiles in reaching Levering's property. Ultimately, development of the land would take five years before Levering was ready to start selling lots.

In 1925, the Valley of the Falls Tract was finally dedicated and officially opened for sale on Saturday, May 30, with a huge barbecue for prospective buyers.[456] One hundred lots, 60 feet wide and 100 to 125 feet deep, with water under pressure from Snow Canyon, would be the first to be offered for sale from the approximately eight hundred available. The opening price per lot was $400.[457] Johnson and Cell realtors in Redlands were the sales agents, but it was noted that E.C. Gird, May's brother, would be in charge of sales in Hollywood, and Gird's twenty-nine-year-old son-in-law, Chester Gillmore, a former service station owner, would be a sales agent in greater Los Angeles.[458] Chester had married Maybelle, Edward C. Gird's daughter and Levering's niece, on October 30, 1912.[459]

Five hundred people responded to the invitation to Levering's celebratory barbecue, despite the difficulty in traveling there, and the *San Bernardino County Sun* newspaper reported enthusiastically on the event. "First sales were registered by Johnson & Cell's forces, with the first lot sold to Frank Erigante of Santa Ana. Twenty lots were sold, with about as many more reserved for prospective purchasers. The customers came from Redlands, San Bernardino, Colton, Santa Ana, Long Beach, Orange and other cities throughout Southern California."

At its opening, Levering's dream in Mill Creek Canyon was still fairly primitive, as neither the electrical utility was in yet[460] nor the paved road completed, but an early purchaser, a Mrs. Stewart, took only four months to build her cabin, which she called "Justamere Inn," where she was serving up fried chicken dinners to the public by September 1925.

Achieving a remarkable feat of persuasion and diplomacy, Levering convinced the other property owners in the canyon to help foot the bill for a new, paved Forest Home Boulevard that would connect his property to

Maybelle Gird. *Courtesy Janice Gillmore private collection.*

town over a distance of seven miles.[461] The chain gang from the prison camp still operating in the lower canyon completed two miles of the road, and the property owners completed the remaining five miles, footing a bill of almost $70,000 by its completion. It was the first and, at the time, the only completely paved road from sea level to six thousand feet in the state.[462]

Levering's wish for resorts was more quickly fulfilled than his work on infrastructure. G.O. "Guy" Swartz, a rancher from Valencia Heights near Covina, and his wife decided to get into the mountain resort business and bought lots for a lodge with a dining room, a store, a delicatessen and ten small housekeeping cabins, which they named Big Falls Lodge Resort.[463] Big Falls Lodge opened on May 29, 1928. At the western end of the tract, lower down the canyon, James A Roulette and his wife built another resort called the Elkhorn Inn. It featured a store, which still exists as the Elkhorn General Store, tent cabins and housekeeping cabins, tennis grounds and shower baths.[464] In 1929, Guy Swartz and Mrs. Roulette got into a pitched battle when they both petitioned the government to have the post office in their stores.[465] Back then, there were no telephones in the canyon[466] and letters were the only means of communication, so mail meant a lot more business for whoever had the post office plus the perk of selling postal supplies. Forest Home, about three miles down the canyon, had been operating a U.S. post office since 1908,[467] which was why Forest Home was the first officially named place in the canyon and the reason the community carried that name for decades. However, three miles was quite a distance then, and residents wanted a second post office. Levering, ever a booster for his development, met with the postal inspector and assured him that a post office at Valley of the Falls would serve two hundred cabins and have an average year-round patronage of at least twenty customers.[468] It's interesting to note that Mrs. Roulette's application requested a post office for "Fallsville," while Mr. Swartz requested one for "Valley of the Falls." The U.S. Post Office denied "Valley of the Falls" as too long a name. However, it granted the post office to Mrs. Roulette's Elkhorn Store and in its wisdom denied the name Fallsville, instead choosing the name Falls Vale, which became contracted to Fallsvale. A new community was born.

The naming of the upper canyon as a separate town meant four distinct communities for Mill Creek Canyon—Igo's, Forest Home, Fallsvale and Valley of the Falls. By today's transportation and communication standards, it seems humorous that there would be four separate villages, two with post offices, plus Torrey's across the creek, Big Pine Resort on

BIG FALLS LODGE --- IN MILL CREEK CANYON
A Place of Spectacular Beauty

BIG FALLS LODGE is easily accessible, located only 18 miles from Redlands, California, within 100 miles of most of Southern California (see map), at an altitude of 6300 feet in one of the few unspoiled areas of natural wilderness in the Southland. In addition to the numerous streams in the immediate area of the Lodge there are several small lakes within riding or hiking distance which afford excellent trout fishing during the season.

Large and small game are plentiful within the area—raccoons, quail, wild pigeons, squirrel, deer, and occasionally a bear or a fox.

The climate at BIG FALLS LODGE is dry, healthful and invigorating and is considered very beneficial to people suffering with arthritic, asthmatic, and sinus conditions.

We, the management of BIG FALLS LODGE expect and encourage our guests to enjoy themselves to the utmost. We want you to forget your formalities and relax in order that your visit with us, whether it be a day, a week, or a month, will do you some good and will long be remembered.

Cabin Rates — European Plan

Daily:
1 or 2 persons..................$5.00 to $6.00
3 or more persons ..$2.00 per person per day

Weekly:
2 place cabins.............................$30.00
4 place cabins........................... 35.00
6 place cabins........................... 45.00
8 place cabins........................... 50.00

15% off weekly rates on reservations of 4 weeks or longer.

(A deposit of 50% is required to assure your reservation.)

Rates for large or small parties during winter months —Oct. 1st to May 1st, quoted on American plan upon request.

MEALS AT POPULAR PRICES

Among mammoth cedars and pines is the Lodge where an array of recreation awaits the guest. In summer—croquet, badminton, ping pong, horse-shoe courts, shuffleboard, dancing, horseback riding, and swimming in a large pool with complete facilities. In winter, the Lodge itself becomes a glorious snow carnival, with skiing, tobogganing, sledding, and ice skating on a beautiful out-of-doors rink.

The Lodge is built of stone and contains a beautiful rustic dining room and lounge where our guests may enjoy plenty of well prepared food selected from menus carrying a large variety at popular prices. Two large fireplaces adorn our dining room and lounge where relaxation and congeniality predominate. Adjoining the dining room is our small rustic cocktail lounge where you may enjoy your favorite drink in an atmosphere of friendship.

At one end and behind the Lodge building, arranged in a picturesque setting, around a beautiful court yard in the center of which is a large fish pond filled with rainbow trout, are nine rustic mountain cottages which will accommodate from 2 to 8 persons. They are completely furnished with innerspring mattresses, gas heat and hot plates, private toilet and lavatory, some with fireplaces. Hot and cold showers are within a few steps of all cottages. All supplies may be obtained at the Lodge store at reasonable prices.

BIG FALLS
CLUB MEMBERSHIPS
ARE NOW AVAILABLE

Inquire for particulars — It's to your advantage

Big Falls Lodge brochure, circa 1930s. *Courtesy Janice Gillmore private collection.*

Coffey Road and Cedar Lodge above Forest Home, but these resort areas were quite separate in 1930. As families opened businesses, children came to live in the canyon year-round. Levering, the former schoolteacher, provided both land and a building across the street from the Elkhorn Inn as an emergency elementary school for the ten children in the community to attend. Edna Johnson was hired as the teacher with the proviso that she would be employed only as long as attendance didn't drop below five pupils.[469] Within two years, a permanent school on land deeded by the Torreys would open.[470]

A sense of foreboding pervades as we watch N.L. Levering through the long lens of time pour his energy and heart into building the Valley of the Falls Tract. The United States would suffer one of the most devastating financial crises in its history and the Great Depression in just a few years. Ineluctably, the 1930s proved to be a challenging decade for Mill Creek Canyon's resorts and communities right from the outset, even for the wildlife. During the winter of 1931, the snow was so deep that the deer were starving and coming to people's homes searching for food. Levering loaded his car with alfalfa, and when he could drive no farther up the canyon, he put the feed on sleds and pulled them to his land to save the deer in Valley of the Falls.[471] He was sixty-two years old. Despite the Depression and aging, nothing seemed to slow Levering down.

It's difficult to discern exactly how the financial crash affected Levering. Outwardly, he and May appeared to still entertain graciously, and Lee persisted in his business enterprises while getting involved with oil exploration and more land development.[472] He kept his hand in politics and remained a devoted club man, belonging to many organizations. However, in August 1933, when the delinquent tax list for San Bernardino County was published, twenty-three owners of lots in the Valley of the Falls Tract were on it. These included Edward C. Gird and his good friends the Van Horns, who had just built a castle-like home across from the falls and several distinctive log cabins that still exist in Forest Falls. N.L. Levering was also delinquent on taxes for hundreds of lots, both improved and unimproved, that had not yet sold.[473] By 1940, he would lose several of those lots in Valley of the Falls to the state for unpaid taxes.[474] While he moved on to other developments, Levering had others supervise the Valley of the Falls Tract, and Chester Gillmore, Levering's nephew-in-law, sold Levering's mountain lots for him from a tiny office in the woods.[475] When George Humphrey, who had subdivided the lots lower down the canyon at Igo's, purchased the last of the old Jackson Ranch below Forest Home and subdivided it in 1939,[476] Gillmore sold those lots. Chester Gillmore Real Estate became Chester Gillmore and Son when Richard "Dick" Gillmore, the younger of Maybelle and Chester's two sons, joined the business in 1948.[477]

Levering had always had political ambitions, and he ran for office in state government as an assemblyman, state treasurer and senator several times, all without success. Although political power had been denied Levering through election, he was finally admitted to the halls of government at the age of seventy when he was appointed clerk of the State of California *Senate Daily Journal*, a post he served in until he was eighty-two. Clearly, Lee Levering never intended to slow down, but his life came to a screeching halt on the evening of January 22, 1957, when he was struck by a car while crossing Colton Avenue near Sixth Street in Redlands and fatally injured. He was eighty-seven years old.

At the time of N.L. Levering's death, more than one hundred years had passed since Daniel Sexton had operated his sawmill and the length of Mill Creek Canyon was owned, if not tamed. The resorts that were a summer haven from the heat in the valley below gave way to a year-

The Van Horn brothers, who built the signature log homes in Forest Falls. *Courtesy Janice Gillmore private collection.*

round community within the span of a decade. On November 1, 1960, the two canyon post offices amalgamated into one, officially creating the community of Forest Falls from the two prior communities, Forest Home and Fallsvale. In 1962, Lucy Levering and the other Levering heirs gave Levering Falls (Big Falls) and sixty acres to the U.S. Forest Service.[478] "Tightening controls of the Falls, which have claimed many lives and trapped numerous hikers, became a possibility when the U.S. Forest

Chester Gillmore's real estate office opened on July 4, 1925. *Courtesy Janice Gillmore private collection.*

George Humphrey's Forest Home Park sales office, 1930s. *Courtesy Janice Gillmore private collection.*

Noah L. Levering at Valley of the Falls Tract, 1920s. *Courtesy Janice Gillmore private collection.*

A fond farewell. *Courtesy Janice Gillmore private collection.*

Service obtained title to the Big Falls property....Ranger Hickerson stated that the property will now become National Forest land, and that the Forest Service can legally control use of the land. He indicated that hikers may be restricted from hiking on Big Falls."

The footprints of the first people to travel and live in the canyon are now all but erased from memory, and the lonesome silence in which David and Mary Ann Frederick first lived at the Mormon mill is lost to the sound of automobiles and airplanes. Mill Creek Canyon, a remote and sometimes inhospitable place of rare and unique beauty, still remains.

NOTES

Introduction

1. Serrano Ancestral Territory map, "Cultural Overview," San Manuel Band of Mission Indians.
2. U.S. Geological Survey, Geographic Names Phase I data compilation (1976–81), December 31, 1981; Jonathan Matti, Douglas Morton, Brett Cox, Scott Carson and Thomas Yetter, "Geologic Setting of the Yucaipa Quadrangle," U.S. Geological Survey, 1992; Forest Falls Quadrangle, State of California Department of Water Resources, U.S. Department of the Interior Geological Survey, 1970.
3. Geographic Names, Big Falls, ID 26984, Forest Falls, U.S. Geographical Survey.
4. W.A. Bryant and M. Lundberg, compilers, U.S. Geological Survey, 2002.
5. "Ships and Shipbuilding in California," *Los Angeles Herald*, January 1, 1895.
6. J.J. Warner, "Reminiscences of Early California from 1831 to 1846," *Historical Society of Southern California*, Los Angeles, California, 1909.
7. "Expediente 99, Spanish Archives," Vignes, 1843, trans. VII, 363–65, MS, California State Archives.
8. J.M. Guinn, *A History of California* (Los Angeles: Historic Record Company, 1907).
9. Scott Harrison, "Ft. Moore Memorial Pays Tribute to Los Angeles Pioneers," *Los Angeles Times*, March 26, 2019.

10. Historic American Engineering Record, Mill Creek 2 and 3 Hydroelectric Systems, H.H. Sinclair Monument, 1926.

11. "Seven Oaks," *Redlands Citrograph* 12, no. 20 (May 27, 1893).

12. "Bear Valley: The Journey Up Mill Creek to Get There, A-Burroback from 'Thurman's'," *Los Angeles Times*, September 5, 1891.

Chapter 1

13. Southern California/Basin: Serrano, John Peabody Harrington papers, National Anthropological Archives, Smithsonian Institution, 1918.

14. John D. Goodman II, archaeologist, interview October 19, 2019.

15. Ruth Benedict, "A Brief Sketch of Serrano Culture," *American Anthropologist* 26, no. 3 (July–September 1924): 368.

16. Edward Gifford, "Clans and Moieties in Southern California," *American Archaeology and Ethnology* 14, no. 2 (March 29, 1918): 177.

17. John Johnson and Joseph Lorenz, "Genetics, Linguistics, and Prehistoric Migrations: An Analysis of California Indian Mitochondrial DNA Lineages," *Journal of California and Great Basin Anthropology* 26, no. 1 (2006): 33–64.

18. Michael Lerch, "Acorns—The California Indian Staff of Life," *Heritage Keepers Newsletter* 2, no. 1, Dorothy Ramon Learning Center (Banning, 2005).

19. John Goodman II and Gina Griffith, "The Mill Creek Recreation Residence Tract: Inventory and Historic Integrity Assessment for the National Register of Historic Places Eligibility Statement," San Gorgonio Ranger District, Front Country, San Bernardino National Forest, San Bernardino County, July 2008, 15.

20. Ernest Siva, interview, Dorothy Ramon Learning Center, Banning, California, October 29, 2019.

21. Russell Thornton, Tim Miller and Jonathan Warren. "American Indian Population Recovery Following Smallpox Epidemics," *American Anthropologist*, New Series 93, no. 1 (1991): 28–45.

22. Paul Spitzzeri, "To Seduce and Confuse: The Rowland-Workman Expedition of 1841," *Southern California Quarterly* 80, no. 1 (Spring 1998).

23. *Craig, Cave et al. vs. Craft et al.*, Testimony of Daniel Sexton, George William Beattie and Helen Pruitt Beattie papers, 1895–1944, Huntington Library, San Marino, California.

24. George Weeks, *California Copy* (Washington, D.C.: Washington College Press, 1928).

25. Harrington in Jeffery Altschul, Richard Ciolek-Torrello, Donn Grenda, Jeffrey Homberg, Su Benaron and Anne Stoll, "Man and Settlement in the Upper Santa Ana Drainage: A Cultural Resources Overview," *Technical Series* 1, Statistical Research Inc. (Tucson: 1984)

26. California State assemblymember James Ramos, Indigenize UCR Teach-In, University of California, Riverside, March 1, 2020.

27. Dorothy Ramon and Eric Elliot, *Wayta' Yawa'* (Banning, CA: Malki Museum Press, 2000).

28. Gary Stickel and Lois Weiman-Roberts, "An Overview of the Cultural Resources of the Western Mojave Desert," United States Department of Interior, Bureau of Land Management, 1980, 98.

29. Burnett in Clifford Trafzer's introduction to the symposium "Killing California Indians: Genocide in the Gold Rush Era," University of California, Riverside, November 7, 2014.

30. "Indian Outrages," *Wilmington Journal*, reported in *Sacramento Daily Union*, August 25, 1866.

31. David Olsen, "Did Native Americans' Deaths Add Up to Genocide?" *Riverside Press Enterprise*, November 8, 2014.

32. Lynn Valbuena, "California's Historic Apology for Native American Genocide Can Start the Healing Process," *Daily Bulletin*, June 29, 2019.

Chapter 2

33. Tom Castro, Daniel Sexton descendant, personal communication, July 23, 2019.

34. U.S. Department of the Interior, Bureau of Land Management, General Land Office Records, Louisiana and Arkansas, 1837–1846.

35. David Burr and John Arrowsmith, Cartographers, *Map of the United States of North America with Parts of the Adjacent Countries*, 1839, Library of Congress.

36. Daniel Sexton, "Letters to the Editor," *Arkansas Times & Advocate* (Little Rock), June 1841, Library of Congress.

37. Doyce Nunis Jr., ed., *The Bidwell-Bartleson Party: 1841 California Emigrant Adventure* (Santa Cruz, CA: Western Tanager Press, 1992).

38. Daniel Sexton, "Letters to the Editor," *Los Angeles Times*, July 2, 1891.

39. Daniel Sexton Sr., U.S. Passport Application, State of Arkansas, County of Desha, 1843, *Fold 3*, courtesy Susan Wyckoff.

40. Ibid.

41. "San Bernardino County, Its Climate and Resources in 1876" in *Ingersoll's Century Annals of San Bernardino County: 1769 to 1904*, Luther Ingersoll, ed. (Los Angeles, 1904); "Cahuilla," Project Gutenberg, *World Heritage Encyclopedia*.

42. Letter from Daniel Sexton to Antonio F. Coronel, December 27, 1885, Antonio F. Coronel Papers, Seaver Center for Western History Research.

43. Donald Chaput, "The Temescal Tin Fiasco," *Southern California Quarterly* 67, no. 1 (Spring 1985): 1.

44. Frank Evans, "The San Jacinto Tin Mines," *Los Angeles Daily Herald*, February 6, 1889.

45. Horace Bell, *Reminiscences of a Ranger; Or, Early Times in Southern California* (Los Angeles: Yarnell, Caystile & Mathes, Printers, 1881).

46. "Acquisition of California: An Interesting Portion of the History of This Part of the State," *Los Angeles Herald*, November 19, 1893.

47. "Death of Senora Domian, Once a Los Angeles Belle," *Los Angeles Herald*, November 3, 1894.

48. Castro, personal communication, June 27, 2019.

49. Scott MacConnell, "Jean-Louis Vignes California's Forgotten Winemaker," *Gastronomica: The Journal of Food and Culture* 11, no. 1 (Spring 2011): 89–92.

50. Annick Foucrier, "Le rêve californien: Migrants français sur la côte Pacifique," XVIIIe–XXe siècles, Histoire et Société (Belin, Paris: 1999).

51. Raymond Clar, *California Government and Forestry: From Spanish Days Until the Creation of the Department of Natural Resources* (Sacramento, CA: Division of Forestry, Department of Natural Resources, 1959).

52. "Expediente 99, Spanish Archives," Vignes, 1843, trans. VII, 363–65, MS, California State Archives.

53. *Santa Cruz County History Journal*, no. 3, Art and History Museum of Santa Cruz County, Santa Cruz, California, 1997.

54. "Tin Mines: The History of One of the Chief Industries of Our County," *San Bernardino Weekly Courier*, February 6, 1892.

55. Rose Ellerbe, "History of Temescal Valley," *Historical Society of Southern California* 11, no. 3 (1920): 12–20.

56. Daniel Sexton, "Letters to the Editor," *Los Angeles Herald*, April 21, 1882.

57. M. Harris Newmark, *Sixty Years in Southern California* (New York: Knickerbocker Press, 1916).

58. "Court of Sessions," *Los Angeles Star* 13, no. 28 (November 14, 1863); "Election of Delegates," *Los Angeles Star* 6, no. 23 (October 18, 1856).

59. "The Pioneers," *Daily Courier* (San Bernardino, CA), April 1, 1888.

60. Register of Deaths, San Bernardino County, 1893/94.
61. Ibid., 1898/99.

Chapter 3

62. W.R. Cross, *The Burned-over District: The Social and Intellectual History of Enthusiastic Religion in Western New York, 1800–1850* (Ithaca, NY: Cornell University Press, 1981).
63. "David Frederick," Family search, the Church of Jesus Christ of Latter-day Saints. Church History Library, Salt Lake City, Utah.
64. Albert Lyman, *Biography of Francis Marion Lyman 1840–1916* (Delta, UT: Melvin A. Lyman Publisher, 1958), 7
65. Lorin Hansen, "Voyage of the Brooklyn," *Dialogue: The Journal of Mormon Thought* (1988): 21.
66. D. Blethen Adams Levy, "Brooklyn," The Maritime Heritage Project— San Francisco, 1846–1899.
67. S.B. Kimball, "The Mormon Battalion March 1846–1847," *Ensign, Church of Jesus Christ of Latter-day Saints* (July 1979).
68. Richard Cowan and William Homer, *California Saints: A 150-Year Legacy in the Golden State* (Provo, UT: Brigham Young University, 1996), 167–84.
69. Kimball, "Mormon Battalion March 1846–47."
70. The Church of Jesus Christ of Latter-day Saints, Church History, Mormon Battalion Sick Detachments, 1847.
71. Edward Lyman, *San Bernardino: The Rise and Fall of a California Community* (Salt Lake City, UT: Signature Books, 1996).
72. Kerry Petersen, David Frederick and Mary Ann Winner, genealogical notes, personal communication, June 28, 2018.
73. John Brown Jr. and James Boyd, *History of San Bernardino and Riverside Counties* I (Madison, WI: Western Historical Association, 1922).
74. Lowell John Bean and Charles Smith, "Cupeño," in *Handbook of North American Indians*, William C. Sturtevant, ed. (Washington, D.C.: Smithsonian Institution, 1978), 8.
75. Scott Partridge, *Thirteenth Apostle: The Diaries of Amasa M. Lyman 1832–1877* (Salt Lake City, UT: Signature Books, 2016). Kindle version.
76. Richard Bullock, *The Ship* Brooklyn *Story, II,* "The Connections Between the Mormon Battalion and the Ship Brooklyn Pioneers," 2008, 12.
77. David Frederick, correspondence, courtesy Kerry Petersen and LDS Church History Archives.

78. Loretta Hefner, "From Apostle to Apostate: The Personal Struggle of Amasa Mason Lyman," *Dialogue* 16, no. 1 (1992): 90–104.

79. Edward Lyman, "The Rise and Decline of Mormon San Bernardino," *BYU Studies Quarterly* 29, no. 4 (1989): 43–63.

80. Lyman (#10), Rich and Frederick (#1) to Bachman Mercantile Mortgage B6, *Los Angeles Star,* June 22, 1858.

81. Selected Pension Application Files Relating to the Mormon Battalion, Mexican War, 1846–48, Frederick, David, Record Group 15, 33, National Archives.

Chapter 4

82. Descendants of Jean Farcy, Generation 5, "Peter Atticus Forsee."

83. "James Forsee, Attorney at Law," *Indianapolis Gazette,* June 19, 1827.

84. List of students, Hanover College, Hanover, Indiana, 1835; "Life of Peter Forsee," *Daily Courier*, December 28, 1888.

85. "Federal Convention of the 16 January: Lawyers," *Democrat*, February 18, 1840; "Peter A. Forsee and Ann Burk," Indiana, Marriages, 1810–2001, Marriage Registration, December 25, 1839.

86. "Moses Burk," 1850 Census, Noblesville, Indiana.

87. "California Pioneers, Alexander Campbell Forsee," *Daily Courier*, December 30, 1888; "Society of Pioneers," *Daily Courier*, January 22, 1888.

88. "Life of Peter Forsee," *Daily Courier*, December 28, 1888.

89. California State Census Records, El Dorado County, 1852, U.S. Federal Census Records, 1850, El Dorado and 1860, Mendocino, "The Pioneers," *Daily Courier*, May 13, 1888.

90. Guinn, *History of California.*

91. "From San Bernardino," *Los Angeles Star*, August 4, 1860; "Indian Affairs," *Los Angeles Star,* July 5, 1862.

92. *Daily Alta California* in the *Times Picayune*, August 13, 1858; Colonel Herbert Hart, USMC, *Historic California Posts: Camp Carleton* (Sacramento: California State Military Museum, 1965).

93. Leonard Taylor and Robert Taylor, *The Great California Flood of 1862* (Redlands, CA: Redlands Fortnightly Club, n.d.).

94. "San Bernardino Correspondence," *Los Angeles Star*, February 22, 1862.

95. J.M. McNulty, Report to Surgeon General U.S. Army, Santa Fe, October 1863, *The War of the Rebellion: A Compilation of the Official Records of the Union*

and Confederate Armies, Series I, L, part II, no. 50.1 (Washington, D.C.: 1897), 137.

96. Edwin Sherman, Letter to General E.V. Sumner, U.S. Army, Commander of the Pacific Division, San Bernardino, June 3, 1861, *The War of the Rebellion: A Compilation of the Official Records of the Union and Confederate Armies*, Series I, Volume L, Part II, No. 50.1 (Washington, D.C.: 1897) , 497.

97. Boyd Finch, "Sanctified by Myth: The Battle of Picacho Pass," *Journal of Arizona History* 36, no. 3 (Autumn 1995): 251–66.

98. "Peter Atticus Forsee," California Great Registers, San Bernardino County, August 26, 1867; "Nelson Van Tassel," 1870 Census, San Bernardino City, San Bernardino County.

99. "Five Years of Crime in California," *Petaluma Weekly Argus*, March 28, 1867.

100. "William Petty," Great Register, Calpella Township, Mendocino County, California 1866; Testimony of William B. Petty, *Tyler vs. Petty*, 13a, 1892, San Bernardino County Historical Archives.

101. "Peter Forsee," *Daily Courier*, December 1, 1886.

102. "Fair Forseeville," *Daily Courier*, August 13, 1887.

103. "Forsee's Camp," *Daily Courier*, July 21, 1887.

104. "Local Brevities," *Daily Courier*, June 17, 1887.

105. Frank Moore, "With a Grain of Salt," *Redlands Daily Facts*, July 19, 1974; "San Bernardino Items," *Los Angeles Herald*, May 27, 1876.

106. Testimony of John Ball, *Tyler vs. Petty*, 1892, 10, San Bernardino County Historical Archives.

107. "Peter A. Forsee, Martha McHaney," Marriage Licenses C, pages 1–320, San Bernardino County Records Archive, February 22, 1878; "William McHaney," 1870 Census, Gallatin, Union Township, Daviess County, Missouri.

108. "Peter A. Forsee," 1880 Census, San Bernardino Township, San Bernardino County, California.

109. "Peter A. Forsee," Wills, Item Book D, Page 66, November 16, 1888, Court Records, San Bernardino County Records Archive.

110. Last Will and Testament of Peter A. Forsee, admitted to probate December 15, 1888, San Bernardino County Historical Archives.

111. In the Matter of the Estate of Peter A. Forsee, Deceased," Probate no. 779, December 1888, San Bernardino County Historical Archives; "Superior Court," *Daily Courier*, February 10, 1889.

112. "He Was a Bad Man," *Los Angeles Times*, April 12, 1895; "Local Brevities," *Daily Courier*, June 1, 8 and 16, 1887.

113. "Frank L. James," Coroner's Inquests 01400–01549, San Bernardino County Records Archive, May 31, 1894.
114. "Chief Martin Is in Charge of the City Police" *San Bernardino County Sun*, June 1, 1917.
115. "A Hilarious Miner Steals a Fifteen-Dollar Kiss," *Los Angeles Times*, December 9, 1897.
116. "Charged with Stealing Cattle," *Los Angeles Times*, April 29, 1892.
117. "San Bernardino County," *Los Angeles Times*, June 25, 1892.
118. "A Mine of Many Millions," *Los Angeles Herald*, March 5, 1895.
119. Ibid.
120. Burr Belden, "History in the Making: Diamonds on His Hat," *San Bernardino County Sun*, July 4, 1957.
121. "Left with Them: Trio of Suspected Counterfeiters Taken to Los Angeles," *Evening Transcript*, March 12, 1900.
122. "Want a Receiver," *Los Angeles Herald*, October 13, 1895.
123. "Handled Counterfeit Money," *Los Angeles Times*, March 11, 1900.
124. "James McHaney Charged with Counterfeiting," *San Francisco Call*, March 11, 1900.
125. "The Public Service—In the Offices and Courts: Summary of the Day," *Los Angeles Times*, September 6, 1900.
126. "Real Estate Transfers," *Daily Courier*, June 8, 1892.
127. "Martha Forsee," *San Bernardino County Sun*, June 13, 1911.
128. "Deaths," *Los Angeles Times*, May 5, 1931.
129. "Bill McHaney of the Old West Goes Out Yonder," *Desert Sun*, January 6, 1937

Chapter 5

130. William Bailey Petty, Ohio, County Births; "Absalom Petty," 1850 Census, Peno, Pike County, Missouri.
131. 1860 Census, Quincy Post Office, Fillmore Township, Plumas County, California.
132. William Bailey Petty, Great Register, San Bernardino County, 1892.
133. William Petty, Great Register, Mendocino County, 1866.
134. Google Maps, directions, Calpella to Ukiah, California, accessed June 12, 2019.
135. Agreement between Peter A. Forsee and William Petty, November 22, 1875, San Bernardino County Historical Archives.

136. Donald Pisani, "Squatter Law in California, 1850–1858," *Western Historical Quarterly* 25, no. 3 (1994): 277–310.

137. "Mr. O'Farrell and the Settlers," *Sonoma Democrat*, August 12, 1858.

138. Original Survey, Township 1S, Range 1W, April 16, 1857, United States Department of the Interior, Bureau of Land Management, General Land Office Records.

139. Edna Monch Parker, "The Southern Pacific Railroad and Settlement in California," *Pacific Historical Review* 6, no. 2 (June 1937): 103–19.

140. Original Survey, Township 1S, Range 1W, June 20, 1896, United States Department of the Interior, Bureau of Land Management, General Land Office Records; Southern Pacific Railroad Company, July 27, 1866: Grant-RR-Atlantic and Pacific (14 Stat. 292), United States Department of the Interior, Bureau of Land Management, General Land Office Records

141. Jerome Madden, "The Lands of the Southern Pacific Railroad Company," S.P.R.R. Company, San Francisco, April 1, 1880.

142. Testimony of William Petty and Lester S. Jenks, *Rachel M. Tyler v. Elizabeth Petty, et al.*, 1892, San Bernardino County Historical Archives.

143. "Elizabeth Archer," birth registry, Schuyler County, Illinois, 1834.

144. "Winston Archer" and "Zadock Jackson," 1850 Census, District Six, Bates County, Missouri.

145. Linda Offerdahl, sketch of the ancestors of Jean (Eugenia) Olive Carlson Offerdahl and Marlin Orville Offerdahl, courtesy of Norma Harvey, great-granddaughter of George and Olive Jackson.

146. Sandra Chase, personal communication, May 26, 2019.

147. Jackson and Archer, California Marriage Index, Sonoma County, 1854.

148. Zadock Jackson, Pacific Coast Directory, Petaluma, Sonoma County, California, 1867.

149. "Jackson, Z." 1870 Census, Lynx Creek, Yavapai County, Arizona Territory.

150. Linda M. Offerdahl, personal family history, undated.

151. "Zadock Jackson," Courts, Probate Minutes D, Page 90, March 23, 1874, San Bernardino County Historical Archives; "Jackson, Richard and Lee," 1880 Census, San Bernardino Township, San Bernardino County.

152. "William Petty and Elizabeth Jackson," Marriages, Marriage Licenses B, 241–480, Item Page 271, San Bernardino County Historical Archives.

153. "San Bernardino Items," *Los Angeles Herald*, May 27, 1876.

154. Truman Reeves, *A Volume of Memoirs and Genealogy of Representative Citizens of Northern California* (Chicago: Standard Genealogical Publishing Company, 1901), 56–57.

155. Ibid.

156. Complaint, *Rachel M. Tyler v. Elizabeth Jackson, et al.*, September 17, 1892, Courts, San Bernardino County Historical Archive; "William B. Petty," Certificate of Death, October 26, 1895, Los Angeles County, California.

157. Judgement, *Rachel M. Tyler v. Elizabeth Jackson*, July 5, 1893, Courts, San Bernardino County Historical Archives; "Elizabeth Petty," Recorder, Deaths, Deaths Book 5, 251–501, item page, 253, September 22, 1893.

158. "William B. Petty," Certificate of Death, October 26, 1895, Los Angeles County, California.

159. George Jackson and Ollie Clemence, Recorder, Marriages, Marriage Licenses D, pages 301–600, item page 406, March 23, 1886, San Bernardino County Historical Archives.

Chapter 6

160. "Sylvanus Thurman," in J.M. Guinn, *A History of California* (Los Angeles: Historical Records Company, 1907).

161. "Charlotte Ann Allison," San Bernardino County Recorder Archive, Marriages B, pages 1–240, item page 37, September 26, 1872.

162. "Mrs. Amanda J. Ball and Sylvanus Thurman," Marriage Registry, California Department of Public Health, Los Angeles County, November 3, 1878; 1870 Census, San Fernando Township.

163. Sylvanus Thurman testimony in *Tyler vs. Petty* water case, 1892–93.

164. Tom Atchley, "The Early Years of Frank Elwood Brown," *Redlands Chronicles*, October 2015.

165. W.H. Hall, "Irrigation in California [Southern]: The Second Part of the Report of the State Engineer of California on Irrigation and the Irrigation Question," California State Printing Office, Sacramento, 1888.

166. Eliza Crafts, *Pioneer Days in the San Bernardino Valley* (Los Angeles: Kingsley, Moles, and Collins Company, 1906).

167. "Old Bear Valley Dam," Office of Historic Preservation, California State Parks.

168. Tom Core, "Bearly Remembered: Pine Knot Resort's Forgotten History," *Big Bear Grizzly*, January 25, 2006.

169. "Mary Abbie Pillsbury, 1865," *One Hundred Year Biographical Directory of Mount Holyoke College 1837–1937*, Bulletin Series 30, no. 5; Alumnae Association of Mount Holyoke College, South Hadley, Massachusetts, 1937; "Sylvanus Thurman, Mary A. Pillsbury," San Bernardino County Records Archive, Marriage Licenses H, pages 1–200, item page 83.

170. "San Bernardino Brevities," *Los Angeles Times*, November 22, 1899.

171. "To Raise Angoras in Big Bear Valley," *San Bernardino County Sun*, September 9, 1913.

172. "Uncle Sam Employs Goats," *San Bernardino County Sun*, February 11, 1909.

173. "Bluff Lake to Be Sold for $16,000," *San Bernardino County Sun*, August 19, 1915.

174. "Big Goat Ranch," *Los Angeles Times*, October 30, 1915.

175. "Mrs. Mary Abbie Thurman," *San Bernardino County Sun*, May 31, 1923.

Chapter 7

176. Barbara Becerra, *One Mile Nearer Heaven* (Lima, OH: Fairway Press, 2001), and personal communication, August 26, 2019.

177. "John Goodson Powell," Great Registers of California, 1867, 1868, 1869, 1870, 1875 and 1880.

178. Powell and Keefer, Western States Marriage Index 1809–2011; Headstone, Pioneer Memorial Cemetery, San Bernardino, California.

179. "Died," *Sacramento Daily Union* 42, no. 7432, March 9, 1872; "Katherine Powell Harvey," California Death Index, 1940–1997.

180. "Robert W. Powell," California Death Index, 1940–1997.

181. "John Goodson Powell," Pioneer Memorial Cemetery, San Bernardino, California, Blk 231, Sp 8.

182. Affidavit of Hannah S. Skinner, *Cave, et al. vs. Tyler, et al.*, July 9, 1897, San Bernardino County Historical Archives.

183. Daniel Sherwood and Jessie Powell, Recorder, Marriages, Marriage Licenses D, 301–600, item page 420, May 20, 1886.

184. "Seven Oaks," *Redlands Citrograph* 12, no. 20 (May 27, 1893).

185. "Skinner's Resort," *Redlands Citrograph* (August 27, 1892).

186. "Friday, September 5, 1890," *Daily Courier*, September 7, 1890.

187. Court filings, *Cave, et al. v. Tyler, et al.*, 1894, Recorder, San Bernardino Historical Archives.

188. Harold Salley, *History of California Post Offices*, 1849–1990 (Lake Grove, OR: 1991).

189. Complaint, *Ben W. Cave, et al. plaintiffs v. George W. Tyler, et al. defendants*, September 18, 1894

190. Affadavit of H.H. Cole, *Cave, et al. v. Tyler, et al.*, sworn July 15, 1897, San Bernardino County Historical Archives.

191. "Several Years Fought in Court," *San Bernardino County Sun*, August 8, 1905.

192. H.S. Skinner, Death Registry, San Bernardino County, January 25, 1901, San Bernardino County Historical Archives.

193. "Tragedy Ends Family Feud of Years," *San Bernardino County Sun*, December 22, 1910.

194. Robert W. Powell, Grace Greenlee, Recorder, Marriages, Marriage Licenses M, pages 201–400, item page 287, March 13, 1901, San Bernardino County Historical Archives; "Powell, male," R.W. Powell, father, G. Greenlee, mother, Recorder, births 2, item pages 101 & 102, January 13, 1902, San Bernardino Historical Archives and 1910 Census Hamilton, Illinois, David F. and Grace Mason, Norman E. Powell, stepson.

195. "Shocking Was Slavery of Woman," *San Bernardino County Sun*, December 25, 1910.

196. "Powell Trial Now Slowly Grinding," *San Bernardino County Sun*, April 5, 1911; "Powell Trial," *San Bernardino County Sun*, December 22, 1910.

197. *State of California vs. Powell* case 11864, January 24, 1911, San Bernardino County Historical Archives.

198. "Mrs. Harvey Is Given Divorce Decree," *San Bernardino County Sun*, June 20, 1911.

199. "Woman Carried Before Big Avalanche," *San Bernardino County Sun*, April 17, 1912.

200. "Mountain Lion Jumps in Front of Automobile," *San Bernardino County Sun*, August 23, 1920.

201. "Auto Traffic Builds Scenic Mountain Road," *Los Angeles Times*, July 26, 1914.

202. George Beattie, "A Highlander in Mill Creek," *San Bernardino County Sun*, June 13, 1913.

203. Gray Bright, interviewed by Barbara Becerra, 1959.

204. "Mountain Home Loss Is Very Severe," *San Bernardino County Sun*, February 3, 1916.

205. "Kate Harvey 'War Bride,'" *San Bernardino County Sun*, July 12, 1918.

206. "Kate Harvey to Stand by Her Brother," *San Bernardino County Sun*, July 15, 1919.

207. "Wounded Woman Chooses Love of Brother," *San Bernardino County Sun*, July 16, 1919.

208. "Kate Harvey in Court to Help Acquit Her Brother," *San Bernardino County Sun*, August 1, 1919.

209. "Seeing San Bernardino in Five Minutes: Bob Powell," *San Bernardino County Sun*, January 24, 1920.

210. "Kate Harvey's Sold and Will Be Subdivided," *San Bernardino County Sun*, September 29, 1926.

211. "Sale of Mountain Home Is Announced," *San Bernardino County Sun*, November 17, 1926.

212. "Eight Starving in Mountains," *San Bernardino County Sun*, January 11, 1937.

213. "Kate H. Howard," 1930 Census, Twenty-Nine Palms Township, San Bernardino County.

214. Kate Howard, death registry, San Bernardino County, July 11, 1944.

215. Robert W. Powell, California Death Index, 1940–97.

Chapter 8

216. "Thomas Robert Akers," Great Register of San Bernardino County, 1892, 1894, 1898.

217. "Richard Jackson," California County Births, Petaluma, Sonoma County, December 21, 1867, and William Petty and Elizabeth Jackson, marriage registry, September 2, 1875, San Bernardino County Historical Archives.

218. Homestead Certificate Number 2876, Application 8214, the Heirs of Elizabeth Petty, deceased, United States Department of the Interior, Bureau of Land Management, General Land Office Records, July 27, 1897.

219. "Richard Jackson, Minnie Belle Akers," Recorder, Marriages, Marriage Licenses I, pages 201–400, item page 216, August 10, 1895.

220. "A Queer Family," *Daily Courier*, August 31, 1892.

221. "Whisky and Laudanum," *Los Angeles Times*, December 24, 1893; "Drunken Beast Assaults Family," *Weekly Sun* (San Bernardino, CA), October 27, 1905.

222. "Suits to Be Tried," *Los Angeles Times*, April 30, 1897; "City News," *Los Angeles Herald*, March 30, 1897.

223. "Disgraceful," *Weekly Courier*, November 26, 1892.

224. "Around Town," *Weekly Courier*, December 3, 1892.

225. "Mt. Grayback Reached by Vivian's," *Los Angeles Times*, July 21, 1897.

226. Crain, Belle and Akers, Thomas, July 7, 1897, Marriage Registry, San Jacinto, Riverside County, California.

227. "To Old Greyback's Summit," *Weekly Sun*, August 7, 1897.

228. Homestead Certificate Number 2863, Application 8192, Thomas R. Akers, United States Department of the Interior, Bureau of Land Management, General Land Office Records, July 27, 1897.

229. "Piped Water for Pumping," *San Bernardino County Sun*, November 9, 1897.

230. "No Jam in His Lunch," *San Bernardino County Sun*, September 14, 1889; "Redlands Record," *Los Angeles Herald*, July 17, 1898; "Whipped," *Evening Transcript* (San Bernardino, CA), September 26, 1900.

231. "Mortgages," *Evening Transcript*, January 15, 1900; "Real Estate," *Weekly Sun*, February 2, 1900.

232. "Winston Archer," 1850 Census, Bates County Missouri, and "William Vivian," 1880 Census, Tulare County, California.

233. "Celebrated Case Comes Tuesday," *San Bernardino County Sun*, July 23, 1905.

234. Tom Atchley presentation.

235. "How Her Nose Was Broken," *Evening Transcript*, January 8, 1901.

236. "Akers: Says That Mrs. Jellison Hit Him 'Plump Across the Nose,'" *Evening Transcript*, January 9, 1901.

237. "Three Years in Various Courts," *San Bernardino County Sun*, April 28, 1903.

238. "Akers to Libby," Land Records, San Bernardino County Recorder, December 1901, San Bernardino County Historical Archives.

239. "Akers to Baldwin," Land Records, Recorder, San Bernardino County Historical Archives.

240. "Answer: Alleges That Mrs. Akers Is an Unfit Custodian of Her Child," *Evening Transcript*, August 28, 1902.

241. "Child Hidden," *Weekly Sun*, November 17, 1905.

242. "Earl Akers to His Aunt," *San Bernardino County Sun*, July 30, 1904.

243. "This Wedding Recalls a Story," *San Bernardino County Sun*, November 15, 1905.

Chapter 9

244. Rachel Melinda Moore, "Illinois, Hancock County, Nauvoo Community Project, 1839–1846," BYU Center for Family History and Genealogy; "John Harvey Moore," Life Sketch by Elaine Johnson.

245. Reminiscences of Rebecca Estella Moore, "Children on the Trail, 1–2." Trail excerpt transcribed from "Pioneer History Collection" available at

Pioneer Memorial Museum (Daughters of Utah Pioneers Museum), Salt Lake City, Utah.

246. "Charles Brent Hancock," Marriages, Rachel Melinda Moore, BYU Nauvoo Community Project.

247. "Charles Brent Hancock," Marriages, Chloe Ann Rawson, BYU Nauvoo Community Project.

248. "Descendants," Charles Hancock, "Hancock and Adams Families," Library of Congress, Collection of Mormon Diaries (1935–38), reel 10, item 1, 44; "Uriah Urban Tyler," in Guinn, *A History of California* II.

249. Melinda Jane Hancock Rawson, autobiographical life sketch, familysearch.org, April 24, 2017.

250. 1870–1940 Census Records, Payson, Utah, San Bernardino and Redlands Township, California

251. "Early Family Member Dies," *San Bernardino County Sun*, March 3, 1943.

252. "The Most Prosperous County in California," *Daily Courier*, March 8, 1888.

253. "Covered Wagon Families," *San Bernardino County Sun*, March 29, 1939.

254. "Elizabeth Ann Tyler," February 10, 1866, Payson, Utah birth records, LDS Church History; "Births," Emery Brainerd Tyler, Urban Amasa Tyler, John Hugh Tyler, Guy Edward Tyler, San Bernardino County Historical Archives

255. "Pots of Gold There, Well Might Be," *San Bernardino News and Free Press*, June 27, 1913.

256. "Tyler," Deaths, San Bernardino County Archives, 1876; "Uriah Urban Tyler," Deaths, San Bernardino County Archives, 1882.

257. "George Tyler," 1880 Census, Colton, San Bernardino County, California.

258. "Colton Will Celebrate Fifty-Second Birthday," *San Bernardino County Sun*, May 28, 1939.

259. "Real Estate Transfers," *Daily Courier*, February 24, 1889.

260. "Tired of Life Major Sterling Shoots Himself Through the Body," *Daily Courier*, January 16, 1892.

261. Tom Atchley, "Mill Creek Mines," n.d.

262. "The Mill Creek Quary, [*sic*]" *Daily Courier*, November 1, 1888.

263. "Redlands: James Gardner Clark Home," *Los Angeles Herald*, February 27, 1892.

264. "A Sunday Fire," *Daily Courier*, April 15, 1890.

265. "Real Estate Transfers: Geo. W. Tyler to R.M. Tyler," *Daily Courier*, June 8, 1892.

266. "Tyler, Rachael" 1900 Census, Redlands Township, Exclusive of Redlands City.

267. Ad, Redlands Business Directory, 1894.

268. "Emery B. Tyler, Attorney," *San Bernardino County Sun*, February 24, 1935.

269. "White Mule Cause of Legal Muddle," *San Bernardino County Sun*, January 13, 1907; "The Truce That Failed," *San Bernardino County Sun*, December 20, 1900.

270. *Cave, et al. v. Tyler, et al.*, Superior Court Records, San Bernardino County Archives.

271. "Monday's Court Calendar: Rachel M. Tyler v. Elizabeth Petty," *San Bernardino County Sun*, May 19, 1895, 3; *Barton Land and Water Company, et al. v. Tyler, et al.*, Court Record, San Bernardino County Archives.

272. "Got Out an Injunction Against Edison Company," *San Bernardino County Sun*, September 14, 1902.

273. Darrell Heinrich, "Mill Creek No. 1: Pioneering Commercial Electric Power," *Hydro Review*, HCI Publications, October 2002.

274. George Beattie, "Origin and Early Development of Water Rights in the East San Bernardino Valley," San Bernardino Valley Water Conservation District, Bulletin no. 4, November 1951.

275. "Some Sales of Real Estate," *San Bernardino County Sun*, April 7, 1903.

276. "Redlight Dens Must Go," *San Bernardino County Sun*, December 25, 1903.

277. "Strayed," *San Bernardino County Sun*, March 17, 1910; "The Time for the Annual Roundup," *San Bernardino County Sun*, April 29, 1905; "George W. Tyler to the Little Georgia M Copper Co.," *Weekly Sun*, November 24, 1899; "Personal," *San Bernardino County Sun*, March 7, 1901.

278. "Social Events," *San Bernardino County Sun*, June 2, 1908.

279. "In the Shadow," *San Bernardino County Sun*, May 29, 1913.

280. "Weird Coincidence Marks Tyler Fire," *San Bernardino County Sun*, December 27, 1913; "Hundreds View Scene of Big Find," *San Bernardino County Sun*, June 28, 1913.

281. "E.B. Tyler Service Set for Tuesday," *San Bernardino County Sun*, May 27, 1935.

282. "Tyler," 1920 Census, Azusa Township, San Bernardino County, California.

Chapter 10

283. "Search for Lost Man in Canyon Thickets," *San Bernardino County Sun*, July 27, 1907.

284. "J.W. Dobbs, Highland Resident," *San Bernardino County Sun*, November 6, 1936.

285. "Dobbs and Bolon," Texas, County Marriage Records, 1817–1965.

286. "Yucaipa People Are Happy," *San Bernardino County Sun*, January 21, 1897.

287. Approve closure of seven abandoned well and mine shafts in Yucaipa Mill Creek area, San Bernardino County Board of Supervisors Clerk of the Board Minutes A-041, May 25, 1959, p. 21, San Bernardino County Historical Archives.

288. "189—Electric Streetlights for the City of Pomona," *History (& Prehistory) of Southern California Edison, 1886 to Date*, Edison International, 2014.

289. John Robinson, "Cyrus Baldwin Southern California Hydroelectric Pioneer," *Los Angeles Corral*, no. 203 (Spring 1996).

290. Ronald Burgess, "Redlands Powers the World—How the San Bernardino Valley Developed Modern Electric Power First," Redlands Fortnightly Club, January 18, 2007.

291. "Redlands Electric Light and Power Company," *Illustrated Redlands*, *Redlands Daily Facts*, 1897.

292. "Piped Water for Pumping," *San Bernardino County Sun*, November 9, 1897.

293. "Around the Court House," *San Bernardino County Sun*, November 12, 1897.

294. David and Jennifer Harris, *Afoot and Afield: Inland Empire: A Comprehensive Hiking Guide* (Berkeley, CA: Wilderness Press, 2009), 11.

295. "Y.M.C.A Camp to Be Big Event," *San Bernardino County Sun*, May 25, 1913.

296. Gary Richardson and Tim Sablik, "Banking Panics of the Gilded Age, 1863–1913," Federal Reserve of Richmond, Federal Reserve History.

297. "Public Record," *Evening Transcript*, March 22, 1902.

298. "He Grants Another Pardon," *Chanute Daily Tribune*, November 27, 1907.

299. "Mrs. New Pardoned," *Iola Record*, November 27, 1907.

300. "Dobbs Family Matters," *San Bernardino County Sun*, January 27, 1901.

301. "Real Estate," *Weekly Sun*, March 21, 1902.

302. "Riverside Gets Two Contracts," *San Bernardino County Sun*, January 7, 1902; "Baldwin's Mill Creek Proposition Is Again Before the Riverside Trustees," *Evening Transcript*, July 11, 1902.

303. "Turning the Plant Over to the City Interferes with Bond Placing," *Evening Transcript*, April 3, 1902.

304. "To Grayback's Snowy Summit," *Evening Transcript*, April 18, 1902.

305. "Miss Baldwin Dead," *Los Angeles Times*, May 5, 1903.

306. "E.C. Curtis Returned Yesterday from a Camping Trip in Mill Creek Canyon," *Weekly Sun*, September 18, 1903.

307. "Official Record," #3, *San Bernardino County Sun*, October 2, 1907.

308. "Baldwin, Cyrus G.," California Death Index, 1905–39.

309. "Highland Happenings," *Weekly Sun*, January 10, 1902.

310. Charles Saunders, *The Southern Sierras of California* (Boston: Riverside Press, Houghton Mifflin, 1923), 149–50.

311. "J.W. Dobbs, Highland Resident," *San Bernardino County Sun*, November 6, 1936.

Chapter 11

312. State of Missouri, County of Livingston, Marriage Registry, January 12, 1880.

313. Ohio Births and Christenings Index, 1774–1973, George John Burris, March 30, 1856; Minnesota Territorial Birth Registry, Elizabeth Lansing Wallace, August 30, 1857.

314. "John Burris," 1880 Census, Rich Hill Township, Livingston County, Missouri.

315. "Burris," 1900 Census, Los Angeles, Los Angeles Township, Los Angeles County, California.

316. "Marble and Granite," *Stone: An Illustrated Magazine* 28, no. 6.

317. Jonathan Matti, Brett Cox and Stephen Iverson, "Mineral Resource Potential of the Raywood Flat Roadless Areas, San Bernardino and Riverside Counties, California," Department of the Interior, United States Geological Survey.

318. 1900 Census, Redlands Township Exclusive of Redlands City, San Bernardino County.

319. "Rich Deposit Will Employ a Thousand Men," *Los Angeles Times*, November 7, 1907.

320. "Better Than Gold," *Los Angeles Times*, May 22, 1910.

321. "Official Record–Deed," *San Bernardino County Sun*, September 4, 1907; "Articles Filed," *San Bernardino County Sun*, October 27, 1907.

322. "Marble Found in San Bernardino," *Los Angeles Times*, September 2, 1907; "California Marble," *Stone: An Illustrated Magazine* 29, no., 464.

323. "Marble," *The Monumental News*, 20, no. 1, January 1908.

324. "Planning More Work," *Los Angeles Times*, November 29, 1908; "Official Record," *San Bernardino County Sun*, April 21, 1909.

325. "Home Industry: Build Marble Working Plant," *Los Angeles Times*, March 7, 1909.

326. "Burris," Los Angeles City Directory, 1908.

327. "To Climb a Hill for a Trophy," *San Bernardino County Sun*, September 11, 1909.

328. "Burris Hill Cup Now in Home of Royalty," *Los Angeles Herald*, October 17, 1909.

329. "Another Victory—The Columbia Scores," *Los Angeles Herald*, September 12, 1909.

330. "Royal Tourist Takes the Cup," *Los Angeles Herald*, October 16, 1909.

331. "Columbia Stock Car Wins Again," *Los Angeles Herald*, September 12, 1909.

332. "Burris Cup Controversy," *Los Angeles Times*, October 17, 1909.

333. "No More Racing in Mill Canyon," *San Bernardino County Sun*, October 23, 1909.

334. "Largest Marble Mill Will Be Started Here," *Los Angeles Herald*, February 21, 1909.

335. "California Marble: The Largest Mill on the Pacific Coast for Los Angeles," *Stone: An Illustrated Magazine* 29, no. 10 (March 1909).

336. "Burris," Los Angeles City Directory, 1908.

337. "Bear Seen in Mill Creek Canyon," *Los Angeles Herald*, September 17, 1909.

338. "Contest Over Marble Claims," *San Bernardino County Sun*, July 9, 1908.

339. "Contest Develops on Yucaipa Valley Land," *San Bernardino County Sun*, November 3, 1916.

340. "Marble Decides Issue," *Los Angeles Times*, March 13, 1917.

341. Frank Moore, "With a Grain of Salt," *Redlands Daily Facts*, July 2, 1975.

342. "Official Records," *San Bernardino County Sun*, February 13, 1926.

343. "Old Quarry in Canyon Again Is Developed," *San Bernardino County Sun*, September 4, 1942.

344. C.A. Logan, "Limestone in California," *California Journal of Mines and Geology* 43)1947): 292–93

345. "Notice to Delinquent Co-Owners," *The Signal*, August 26, 1937.

346. "Arthur F. Burris," California Death Index, 1905–1939.

347. "George John Burris," 1910 Census, Los Angeles Township, Los Angeles County.

348. "Burris Is to Ride," *Los Angeles Times*, June 4, 1908; "Burris Loses Pet Columbia," *Los Angeles Times*, February 21, 1911.

349. "Fast Time Is Made on Trip to Southland," *San Bernardino County Sun*, April 13, 1919.

350. Burris, Oscar V., Los Angeles City Directory, 1918.

351. Charles W. Burris, July 24, 1973, Oscar V. Burris, August 27, 1971, California Death Index, Sacramento County.

352. Georgia L. Neis, California Death Index, Los Angeles County, December 19, 1981; Earl R. Burris, California Death Index, Alameda County, March 4, 1984.

353. George J. Burris, California Death Index, Los Angeles County, July 26, 1942; Elizabeth L. Burris, California Death Index, Los Angeles County, July 30, 1947.

Chapter 12

354. "Daniel Rhea Igo," Ohio, Births and Christenings Index, 1774–1973; Allan Whitney, "D. Rhea Igo," *Golden Jubilee: Redlands California 1888–1938*, Citrograph Printing Company (Redlands, 1938); "Benjamin Franklin Igo," December 12, 1889, Ohio, Births and Christenings Index, 1774–1973.

355. Mary Elizabeth Rhea and Daniel Frederick Igo, July 21, 1886, Trumbull County, Ohio, Ohio Marriages, 1800–1958.

356. "Igo vs Igo," Court Case #6163, August 13, 1895, San Bernardino County Historical Archives.

357. Allan Whitney, "D. Rhea Igo," *Golden Jubilee: Redlands California 1888–1938* (Redlands, CA: Citrograph Printing Company, 1938).

358. "Mary E. Igo," 1910 Census, Redlands, San Bernardino County, California.

359. "Daniel Rhea Igo and Maude Agnes Wilkins," San Bernardino County Recorder, Marriage Licenses 1, May 4, 1910, item page 7, San Bernardino County Historical Archives.

360. "Forest Home Has Thrifty Trapper," *San Bernardino County Sun*, January 21, 1911.

361. "Auto Trip to Forest Home," *San Bernardino County Sun*, July 27, 1911.

362. "Resort and Automobile Owners Dream Highway," *Los Angeles Times*, May 1, 1910.

363. "Mill Creek Fourth," *San Bernardino County Sun*, March 30, 1913.

364. "County Warrants for the Month of July," *San Bernardino County Sun*, September 12, 1912.

365. "County Warrants," *San Bernardino County Sun*, November 22, 1913.

366. "Rock Pile May Be Moved to Bear Valley," *San Bernardino County Sun*, September 11, 1913.

367. "Axe Poised for Two Heads in Jail Camps Booze Row," *San Bernardino County Sun*, June 16, 1914.

368. "Mill Creek Camp Opens," *San Bernardino News*, March 3, 1916; "County Library Reports," *San Bernardino County Sun*, January 1, 1930.

369. "Strike Is Broken," *Los Angeles Times*, March 12, 1915; "Convict at Mill Creek Camp Flees," *Los Angeles Times*, August 10, 1923; "A Sickening Orgy Said to Have Taken Place in Mill Creek Prison Camp—Probed," *San Bernardino County Sun*, April 20, 1915; "'Murdered' Man Is Located at Prison Camp," *San Bernardino County Sun*, May 28, 1921.

370. United States Department of the Interior, Bureau of Land Management, General Land Office Records, patent no. 708755, Los Angeles, September 27, 1919.

371. "A Million from Novels," *Literary Digest* 56 (March 2, 1918).

372. "Harold Bell Wright Brings Divorce Suit," *Los Angeles Times*, December 7, 1917; Redlands Historical Timeline Story Map, Redlands Historical Society, ARC GIS, ESRI.

373. Harold Bell Wright, *The Eyes of the World* (Chicago: Book Supply Company Publishers, 1914).

374. "Talkie Version of 'Eyes of the World' Retains Dramatic Appeal," *San Bernardino County Sun*, October 18, 1930.

375. "Donald Crisp, Director," IMdB, https://www.imdb.com; "Regret Note," *Los Angeles Times*, September 22, 1916.

376. Harold Bell Wright Papers 1890–1946, Special Collections, University of Arizona; "Novel Brings Him Fortune," *Los Angeles Times*, November 14, 1909.

377. Tom Atchley, "Igo's and Mountain Home Village," n.d.

378. Mill Creek Canyon Park subdivision map, 1923.

379. "Igo, Humphrey Sell Interest in Mill Creek Park Tract," *San Bernardino County Sun*, December 5, 1929.

380. "Boosters for New Mountain Road at Work," *San Bernardino County Sun*, November 4, 1939.

381. "Cabin Cave-in Kills Man; Eight Injured," *Los Angeles Times*, January 2, 1937.
382. "Canyon Swept by Water and Cabins Ruined," *San Bernardino County Sun*, March 4, 1938.
383. "Death Claims D. Rhea Igo of Mill Creek," *San Bernardino County Sun*, November 27, 1947.
384. "No Longer Igo's," *Redlands Daily Facts*, June 30, 1964.

Chapter 13

385. "Ira Torrey," 1860 Census, Saratoga Township, Marshall County, Illinois.
386. "Death of Charles Wesley Torrey," *La Crosse Chieftain*, March 18, 1898.
387. "Charles W. Torrey," 1880 Census, Sheridan Township, Linn County, Kansas.
388. "Prescott Items," *Linn County Clarion*, December 23, 1892.
389. "Local and Other News," *Prescott Eagle*, January 15, 1887; "Prescott," *Pleasanton Observer*, December 5, 1891.
390. "Louie E. Torrey," California Voter Registration, Long Beach, August 28, 1890.
391. "Prescott Notes," *Linn County Clarion*, May 8, 1891.
392. "Probate Court News," *Linn County Clarion*, December 2, 1892.
393. "Prescott Items."
394. "Facts & History," City of Long Beach Visitors and Convention Bureau.
395. "L.E. Torreys Note 61 Years of Marriage," *Redlands Daily Facts*, December 3, 1953.
396. "Auto Truck Accident," *Los Angeles Herald*, September 15, 1909.
397. "Car Overturns Truck," *Los Angeles Times*, January 25, 1911.
398. "Strikes Van; Injures Two," *Los Angeles Times*, January 25, 1911.
399. "Louie E. Torrey," Long Beach, California city directory, 1914; "Long Beach," *Los Angeles Times*, September 9, 1912; "Louie E. Torrey [Jr.]," Long Beach, California city directory, 1913.
400. "Married on Top of Mountain," *San Bernardino News*, June 5, 1917.
401. Passenger List of Organizations and Casuals, Company "A" 160th Infantry, 40th Division, *Mentor*, August 8, 1918, Brooklyn, New York.
402. "Margaret Clark Torrey," Births 7, Pages 1–154, Page 94, San Bernardino County Historical Archives.
403. 1930 Census, Los Angeles & Los Angeles and Long Beach city directories, 1920, 1921, 1945.

404. "Anna J. Peters and Louie E. Torrey," Los Angeles County Index to Marriages, March 31, 1919; "Nancy Cassidy Furbee and Louie Ellsworth Torrrey," Orange County Marriage Index, January 24, 1952.

405. Records of the Meuse-Argonne Offensive, United States National Archives and Records Administration.

406. "Soldiers Coming Saturday," *Los Angeles Times*, April 10, 1919, 14.

407. "Charles E. Torrey," 1920 U.S. Federal Census, Unincorporated Redlands Township, sheet 1.

408. "Locals," *Covina (CA) Argus*, September 11, 1925, 8.

409. "Trout Breakfast at Forest Home," *San Bernardino County Sun*, May 28, 1915.

410. "Forest Home, a Real Mountain Resort," *Los Angeles Times*, June 9, 1918.

411. Patent #809951, Los Angeles, United States Department of the Interior, Bureau of Land Management, General Land Office Records, June 13, 1921.

412. "Official Records," *San Bernardino County Sun*, April 29, 1924.

413. "Charles Philip Torrey," California, Birth Index, 1923.

414. Gayle Crisfield, cousin, personal interview, October 15, 2019.

415. "Buerger's Disease," Mayo Clinic, http:/www.mayoclinic.org/buerger's disease, accessed October 15, 2019.

416. "Louie E.Torrey," 1930 Census, Redlands Township, San Bernardino National Forest.

417. Deed, Louie E. Torrey and Maggie D. Torrey to Fallsvale School District, San Bernardino County Recorder, Book 745, p 93, official record, San Bernardino County Historical Archives.

418. "Schools Open Tomorrow in 15 Districts," *San Bernardino County Sun*, September 18, 1932.

419. Wallace Fagerstedt, personal interview, April 6, 2016.

420. "Property Toll $500,00 in Eastern Mountains," *San Bernardino Daily Sun*, March 7, 1938.

421. Pauline L. Smith as told to Gayle Crisfield, October 2019.

422. "Canyon Swept by Water and Cabins Ruined," *San Bernardino County Sun*, March 4, 1938.

423. "Church Group Buys Famous Forest Home," *San Bernardino Daily Sun*, July 2, 1938.

424. "Torrey Comes to Defense of Resort Plans," *San Bernardino County Sun*, July 9, 1938.

425. "Redlands Men Join Fight to Avert Permit," *San Bernardino County Sun*, July 8, 1938.

426. "State Denies Liquor Permit in Timberland," *San Bernardino County Sun,* May 9, 1939.

427. Irene Elizabeth Smith Armstrong, sister-in-law of Charles Philip Torrey, as told to her daughter, Gayle Crisfield, October 15, 2019.

428. Mrs. Pansy Jacinto, personal interview, 2014.

429. Jim Turpin, personal interview, July 2012.

430. "Slot Machines Bring Fines to Fallsvale Men," *San Bernardino County Sun,* July 6, 1949.

431. "Torrey's Frosty Lane," Redlands Business Directory, 1944, courtesy Gayle Crisfield.

432. Gayle Crisfield, personal communication, October 16, 2019.

433. "Charles Torrey Promoted in Foreign Service," *Redlands Daily Facts,* May 30, 1966; "Civilian Plane Spotters Cited," *San Bernardino County Sun,* July 26, 1942.

434. "Charles E. Torrey, April 11, 1954," U.S., Headstone Applications for Military Veterans, 1925–1963.

435. "Torrey," *San Bernardino County Sun,* November 6, 1956.

436. "Mrs. Torrey Passes Away," *Redlands Daily Facts,* July 12, 1957.

437. "Louie E. Torre [*sic*] Dies at 94," *Redlands Daily Facts,* October 16, 1959.

Chapter 14

438. "Redlands—To Open New School," *Los Angeles Times,* October 4, 1904; "Golden Is This Wedding," *Los Angeles Times,* August 5, 1905.

439. Lorrin Morrison, "Noah Levering: A Biographical Sketch," *Historical Society of Southern California Quarterly* 40, no. 3, 211–22.

440. Ibid.; The Society's Birthplace, November 1, 1883 (September 1958), 211–22.

441. "Noah Levering," 1870 Census, Lee Summit post office, Jackson County, Missouri.

442. "Noah Levering," 1880 Census, Ballona Township, Los Angeles, California.

443. "Former Newsboy Proud of Anniversary Issue," *Los Angeles Times,* December 5, 1931.

444. "Commencements—The Normal School," *Los Angeles Herald,* June 28, 1890; Paul Spitzzeri, "Getting Schooled at the Los Angeles State Normal School, ca. 1890s," the Homestead Museum.

445. "Real Estate Transfers," *Los Angeles Herald*, June 18, 1896, July 10, 1896, December 29, 1897; *Los Angeles Times*, May 14, 1895, May 9, 1896, June 3, 1896; "Mortgages Over $1,000," *Los Angeles Herald*, February 16, 1898, April 30, 1898; "Personal News—N.L. Levering of the Firm of Levering Bros.," *Los Angeles Times*, July 6, 1890.

446. "Notes and Personals," *Los Angeles Times*, October 13, 1895.

447. City of Redlands, History and Landmarks, https://www.cityofredlands.org/history-landmarks.

448. "Philip Royar," 1900 U.S. Federal Census, Los Angeles Township, Los Angeles County, California.

449. Carey McWilliams, *Southern California: An Island on the Land* (Salt Lake City, UT: Gibbs-Smith Publisher, 1973).

450. Janice Gillmore, great-granddaughter of Edward C. Gird, personal interview, January 2012.

451. "Redlands Brevities," *Los Angeles Times*, August 26, 1902.

452. "Redlands," *Los Angeles Times*, June 6, 1910.

453. "Big Deal in Mountain Land," *San Bernardino County Sun*, November 16, 1920.

454. "Official Records," *San Bernardino County Sun*, February 13, 1926.

455. "Work to Start on Big Project," *Los Angeles Times*, January 29, 1922.

456. "New Mountain Tract to Open," *San Bernardino County Sun*, May 26, 1925.

457. Valley of the Falls Tract advertisement, *San Bernardino County Sun*, September 6, 1925.

458. "Chester Gillmore," 1920 Census, Los Angeles City, Los Angeles County, California.

459. "Society," *Los Angeles Times*, November 3, 1912.

460. "Power Corporation to Build Line into Valley of the Falls Resort," *San Bernardino County Sun*, March 13, 1928; "Large Mountain Subdivision to Be Opened Soon," *Los Angeles Times*, June 14, 1925; Valley of the Falls Tract advertisement, *San Bernardino County Sun*.

461. "Mill Creek Road Completed," *San Bernardino County Sun*, June 12, 1926.

462. "Valley Joins in Road-Day-O in Mill Creek," *San Bernardino County Sun*, August 6, 1926.

463. "Valencia Heights Man Opens Mountain Resort," *Covina Argus*, May 18, 1928.

464. "Milk Creek Resorts," *San Bernardino County Sun*, July 10, 1930.

465. "Close Survey for Redlands Postal Block," *San Bernardino County Sun*, August 16, 1929.

466. "New Telephone Line Is Built for Canyon," *San Bernardino County Sun*, July 12, 1938.

467. "Forest Home, San Bernardino," *United States Official Postal Guide*, U.S. Government Printing Office, Washington, D.C., January 1908.

468. "Close Survey for Redlands Postal Block," *San Bernardino County Sun*, August 16, 1929.

469. "Elementary School Established for Forest Home Area Students," *San Bernardino County Sun*, October 11, 1930.

470. "Schools Open Tomorrow in 15 Districts," *San Bernardino County Sun*, September 18, 1932.

471. "Dear, Dear! Deer Feed's Dear!" *Los Angeles Times*, December 6, 1931.

472. "Fine Home Sites," *San Bernardino County Sun*, April 26, 1931.

473. "Delinquent Tax List—Fallsvale," *San Bernardino County Sun*, August 14, 1933.

474. "Legal Advertisement," *San Bernardino County Sun*, March 13, 1940.

475. "Sees Deer King Upset by Youth," *San Bernardino County Sun*, November 25, 1936.

476. "Forest Home Tract Approved by Board," *San Bernardino County Sun*, July 1, 1939.

477. "Our History," Gillmore Real Estate, Forest Falls, California.

478. "Levering Heirs Turn Big Falls over to U.S. Forest Service," *Redlands Daily Facts*, Redlands, California, January 11, 1962.

ABOUT THE AUTHOR

S hannon Wray's story in Mill Creek Canyon began when her great-great-grandfather went with a U.S. Army detachment to cut trees there for a flagpole at Fort Moore in Los Angeles in 1847. Hailing from a Hollywood family, her aunt was Fay Wray, classic film star of *King Kong* fame. As a young child, she spent every summer in Mill Creek Canyon then moved there year-round in 1968 and attended school at the old two-room stone Fallsvale Schoolhouse. Shannon enjoyed careers in publishing in the United States and Canada before becoming a television producer and traveling the world for national networks for over thirty years. Returning to her hometown in 2009, she became fascinated with the people in its past and now presents the history of the canyon locally. Ms. Wray lives in a historic home in Mill Creek Canyon with her family.

Visit us at
www.historypress.com
....